The Profitability Test

The Profitability Test

Does Your Strategy Make Sense?

Harborne W. Stuart Jr.

The MIT Press
Cambridge, Massachusetts
London, England

This book was set in Stone Sans and Stone Serif by Toppan Best-set Premedia Limited. Printed and bound in the United States of America.

Library of Congress Cataloging-in-Publication Data

Names: Stuart, Harborne W., Jr., author.
Title: The profitability test : does your strategy make sense? / Harborne W. Stuart, Jr.
Description: Cambridge, MA : MIT Press, 2016. | Includes bibliographical references and index.
Identifiers: LCCN 2016008330 | ISBN 9780262529402 (pbk. : alk. paper)
Subjects: LCSH: Business planning. | Marketing.
Classification: LCC HD30.28 .S783 2016 | DDC 658.4/012—dc23 LC record available at
   https://lccn.loc.gov/2016008330

10 9 8 7 6 5 4 3 2 1

To Cathy

Contents

Acknowledgments   ix

Introduction   xi

I   Value Creation and Competition   1

1   Value Creation: The Foundation of Profitability   3

2   Contributed Value and Unrestricted Competition   7

Appendix: The Mathematics of Unrestricted Competition   20

3   Willingness to Pay and Economic Cost   25

Appendix: Using Decision Trees in WTP and Economic-Cost Calculations   39

II   Being Better—Winning the Customer   43

4   Competing for the Customer: The Value-Gap Advantage   45

5   Customer Tastes and Profitability   53

Appendix: Contributed Value and Value-Gap Advantages   58

III   Being in Demand   61

6   Guaranteed Profitability: The Power of Exclusion   63

Appendix: Monopoly Power and Supply-Demand Reasoning   69

7   Envy Is a Form of Exclusion   79

8   Nonconstant Marginal Costs   85

9   Market-Price Effects   95

10   Being in Demand: Guaranteed and Potential Profitability   103

Appendix: Supply and Demand Revisited   109

11   Profitability under Unrestricted Competition   113

IV   Your Firm's Game   115

12   Buyers and Competitors   117
13   Suppliers   127
14   Larger Games   139
15   Economic Value: Relative and Subjective   147

V   Changes in the Game   155

16   Sustaining Profitability   157
17   Strategic Moves: Changing the Game   169
Appendix: Game Matrices for Game Trees   188
18   Strategic Moves: Restrictions   191
Conclusion: A Coherent Story   195

Notes   199
Index   203

Acknowledgments

The research behind this book started as a joint project with Adam Brandenburger. We had the simple, but not well-defined, goal of applying game theory to business strategy. We had no idea at the time that it would shift the study of business strategy away from a zero-sum perspective of beating competitors to an understanding that profits are typically part of some larger value creation. Four people played prominent roles in the early development of this work. Scott Borg helped us understand the broader cultural implications of our approach and was instrumental in developing some of the first teaching materials for our work. Ken Corts also was a partner in developing teaching materials. More important, he patiently helped me make connections to existing theory and was always willing to comment on my papers that developed the theory in this book. Finally, the importance of treating prices as a consequence of competition owes much to the research of Louis Makowski and Joe Ostroy. And I am grateful for the patient encouragement Louis and Joe have provided me through the years.

If this book can be said to have a pre-history, then Howard Raiffa and Vijay Krishna would figure prominently. My suggestion to incorporate cooperative game theory into business strategy turned out to be the essential insight, and I am convinced that this idea is due to these two professors. Vijay taught me cooperative game theory, and Howard's use of cooperative game theory in negotiation led me to apply it to business strategy. Both were wonderful teachers—I feel truly fortunate to have been a student in their classes. And I will forever be thankful to Howard and the late Myron Fiering for their help in launching my academic career.

Because this book, and the theory behind it, has been many years in the making, the people who have provided support and encouragement, both directly and indirectly, are too numerous to name. They include friends, former colleagues, and former students at Harvard Business School, MIT's Sloan School, NYU's Stern School, and

Columbia Business School, as well as current colleagues and students in Columbia Business School's DRO department and Columbia's IEOR department. I especially want to thank some of my friends and colleagues who have provided support specific to the content in this book. They include Amar Bhide, David Collis, Pankaj Ghemawat, Bruce Greenwald, Patrick Sileo, Brian Silverman, and Pai-Ling Yin. And, more generally, I'd like to thank Elon Kohlberg for inspiring me to find the simple, essential insight in anything I try to teach.

The gap between the idea of a book and the actual writing of a book is vast. My decision to write a book was prompted by two former students, Lex Douze and Philipp Kobus. Though this book differs from their original vision of what was needed, they are the original instigators. Cory Williamson put the first words to paper and saved me from the terror of the blank page. I am indebted to him for his efforts. For over twenty years, Rena Henderson—at the risk of mixing metaphors—has been a verbal alchemist. I still marvel at the improvements her editing yields. In the final steps toward publisher acceptance, Marvin Lieberman, Steve Brams, and Dan Raff provided invaluable advice. I am grateful that John Covell at MIT Press, and his successor Emily Taber, understood and appreciated the purpose of this book, and I thank Dana Andrus for her help in producing the final version.

Finally, for the support that matters the most, I'd like to thank my two sons, Hobey and Lawrence, a longtime friend, Jean de Valpine, and my late mother, who sadly just missed seeing the final version. Most important, this book is dedicated to my wife, Cathy, who truly understands dealing with original thoughts.

Introduction

Why is your company profitable? The obvious answer is that your revenues exceed your costs. But why is that the case? In particular, why hasn't competition driven your profits down to zero? Why haven't competitors stolen your customers? You might be surprised that managers rarely can offer a coherent reason for why their company is profitable. They might implicitly understand why, but without an explicit understanding, their company is at risk of making dramatic strategic blunders. For proof of this fact, just think of the last time you read about a company making a major strategic move—say, entering a new market, introducing a new product, or making an acquisition—and you thought, "What were they thinking?" More likely than not, the company had no coherent story for why it was profitable. If they had had such a story, your response probably would have been something like "Good move" if they were successful or "They made the wrong bet" if they failed. But if you're wondering what they were thinking, chances are that they simply *weren't*.

This book is designed to put you in the best possible position to eliminate what-were-you-thinking blunders. It will teach you how to understand profitability so that you can provide logically coherent answers to questions such as: Will your new venture be profitable? Will a change in your company's strategy generate an increase or decrease in profits? If you "stay the course" in your existing business, will you continue to be profitable?

But understanding profitability is more than just a matter of eliminating what-were-you-thinking blunders. Let me state the need bluntly: just because you have a good idea doesn't mean you'll make any money. And if you are making money today, there's no guarantee you'll be making any tomorrow. Quite simply, without an understanding of profitability, in particular, the reason for *your* company's profitability, you could be risking the success of your company or venture without even knowing it.

Traditionally, understanding profitability has been one of the goals of business strategy. For instance, business strategy books typically consist of an expert or "guru" offering frameworks and insights into how to be successful in business. The authors assume that if you follow their advice, you will be profitable.

Here, we will take a very different approach. First and foremost, you, the reader, are the expert on your own business. As the person actually doing business, you are in the best position to make the difficult judgments. You will have to make many assessments, including who your target buyers are; what their tastes are; what new products or technologies you and your competitors might develop or discover; how your employees like working for you; who will decide to compete with you, and how fiercely they will compete. In this book, I will show you how to turn these judgments into a coherent analysis of whether or not you will continue to be profitable, or whether or not an anticipated change in strategy will be profitable. I can't tell you how to run your business—in fact, no outside advisor can—but I can help you make sure that your plan makes as much sense as possible, given your best judgments. If you read this book carefully and apply the concepts that I introduce, you will come away with a coherent story to explain why you will be profitable.

To help ensure that your strategic plans are logically coherent, I present state-of-the-art theory for understanding business strategy from an economic perspective. The theory has its roots in joint work that I did with Adam Brandenburger when we were both on the faculty at Harvard Business School. Although this theory has been part of the MBA curriculum at many business schools—including Harvard, MIT, Columbia, and NYU—and parts of it have been taught for nearly twenty years, this is the first time that the ideas have been written down in an accessible form.

I wrote this book for students of business, whether they are students enrolled in courses or practitioners hungry for a deeper understanding of the business environment. Thus, I will ask you to take on two roles as you read this book. First, I'll ask you to read this book as a business person, always keeping your own personal business context in mind. I present theory, which will often require simplifications and abstractions. I'll ask you to be constantly thinking about how to connect these abstractions to your real world. Second, I'll ask you to approach this book as a student. There will be times when you will want to go slowly and carefully through parts of this the book in order to be sure that you grasp the theoretical concepts. (For the adventurous reader, many chapters have optional appendixes that discuss some of the mathematics behind the theory. These sections are not required for understanding the main ideas.) If you take these two roles seriously, I guarantee you that your efforts will be rewarded many times over.

The main reward will be to understand that *there are only three ways for a company to be profitable*:

1. it must be better than its competitors, or
2. there must be excess demand, or
3. there must be restrictions to competition.

If this seems obvious to you, you might think that you do not need to read this book. But let me give you a sense of what this simple summary, though loosely accurate, leaves out.

1. Being "better" than your competitors does not necessarily mean that you have to have a better product. Nor does it mean that you have to have lower cost. In this book, you will learn what "better" really means in this context.

2. To benefit from excess demand, there does not necessarily have to be excess demand for your product. There are times when excess demand for your competitors' product will guarantee your firm profitability. And it might even be the case that the buyers creating the excess demand have absolutely no interest in your product. This book will give you an understanding of how competition can work in surprisingly indirect ways.

3. Suppose that you are not better than your competitors and that there is no excess demand in your markets. Under these two conditions, you cannot make a profit if competition is unrestricted—that is, if everyone can and does compete aggressively. But firms do make profits when these two conditions hold, as there may be restrictions in the competitive environment. After reading this book, you'll better understand whether your firm's profits can withstand the force of competition: If the restrictions disappear, will your profits disappear, as well?

In part I, I introduce two key principles that you will rely on throughout the book. First, *profits are just a piece of some larger economic pie*. Understanding which people and companies make up the larger economic pie is a key aspect of the art of business strategy—a topic we'll discuss in part IV. But our building block will be a relatively small economic pie—the value that is created when a buyer and seller do a deal. We'll start with the most fundamental of transactions, the buyer–seller deal, with the buyer as the customer and the seller as the company. In the simplest of terms, for a company to be profitable, there must be a favorable deal to be made with each and every customer.

The other key principle is that *prices are typically a consequence of both competition and bargaining*. In this second principle, the important word is "both." You know of situations in which competition alone determines the price of a product. For example, although there is a slight difference between the buying and selling prices of gold, there is effectively one market price determined by supply and demand—that is, by competition. You also know of situations in which the competition has almost nothing to do with the price you pay—think of bargaining at a flea market or a yard sale. Thus, at one extreme, are situations in which competition exactly determines everyone's profits. At the other extreme are situations in which competition has no effect on players' profits—profits will be based only on the players' bargaining or negotiation skills. But many, if not most, business contexts lie between these two extremes. Competition will put some limits on the possible prices that will be paid and received, but bargaining will also be involved in determining the actual prices.

In parts II and III, you'll see how to put these principles to work. In part II, I describe how to be profitable when you have to compete for customers. By focusing on the economic pie created with a customer, you'll see what it means to be better than your competition. To be profitable, you need neither the best product nor the lowest cost product. Moreover, even if you do have the best product, that in itself doesn't guarantee profitability. Similarly, the lowest cost product doesn't guarantee you any profits either. The key is that the *value* you create with your customer must be larger than the value that any other firm can create with your customer. This is a mouthful, but the logic is straightforward: to be profitable, you need customers. To have customers in a competitive situation, you need to win them. And to win them, you have to create more value with them than any other competitor can.

The value you can create with a customer depends on the customer's preferences for your company's product. Thankfully, customers differ in their tastes, and part II concludes by discussing the importance of classifying customers according to their tastes, a process that marketing professionals call segmentation. You'll find that to be profitable, it is useful for a company to identify customer segments in which it is the best at jointly creating value with the customer.

In part III, we'll consider the fortuitous case of excess demand. In such cases, your firm will be on the "right" side of the market, and so understanding profitability would seem almost trivial. However, though fortuitous, the situation is not simple. The existence of excess demand implies capacity limitations, and with capacity limitations, market-price effects arise. Although these effects will usually benefit your firm, they are not immediately obvious. As noted above, your firm could be profitable due to buyers who would not buy your product at any price.

In part IV, you will learn how to apply the analysis to your own situation. This is where you have to draw on your judgments about the business you are in. At a practical level, you will have to make assessments about how buyers and competitors view your firm and its products, and, for at least some of your suppliers, how they assess the cost of serving you. At a theoretical level, you will be learning how to create your own business game. To a game-theorist, parts I through III describe how to model a business context as a game in *characteristic-function form*. While this term is not particularly illuminating, what such a game consists of *is*. A game in characteristic-function form has just two ingredients: people and the value that they can create. And we analyze such a game with unrestricted competition. People, value, and competition—it shouldn't surprise you that a game with these ingredients fits business so well.

Part V addresses some dynamic issues. Besides understanding how other players view your firm, there is another type of judgment that you'll have to make. You will have to assess how the situation might change—in other words, whether the game might change. Relatedly, you'll have to decide whether you *want* to change the game. There are two ways in which your game could change. External factors such as cultural changes in taste or rising commodity prices could affect buyer preferences and costs, respectively. But the game could also change due to the actions of one or more of the existing players. For instance, you or a competitor could expand capacity, develop a new product line, leave an existing market, and so on. Or perhaps a new player could enter one of your markets—that is, a new player could enter the game. We call such actions strategic moves, and in part V, I'll show you how to integrate strategic moves into our theory of value creation and competition.

We use strategic moves in three different ways. First, we use them to help us address two fundamental questions in business strategy: Is our current (or planned) profitability sustainable over time? Can we benefit by changing the game? Second, you'll learn how strategic moves, when applied to our theory of value and competition, can tell us when the "invisible hand" will or will not work. In particular, we will see that the need for management is virtually inevitable in many markets.

Finally, strategic moves let us address the third way in which a company can be profitable: restrictions to competition. Unfortunately, there is no general theory for contexts in which competition is restricted. If your profits are due to some restrictions, then the best you can do is model what the players might do given these restrictions. I provide some examples to show you how this is done. (As an aside, when you see the phrase "game theory" in the popular press, the author is most likely describing a theory of strategic moves and not a theory of value creation and competition.)

When you're done reading this book and seeing how to apply its concepts, it will be time for you to create your own coherent story for your firm's profitability. You will now have the tools to do this, but for those of you needing a gentle nudge to get started, I include a framework that I give my students as an aid to creating their own coherent story.

Let's get started.

I Value Creation and Competition

1   Value Creation: The Foundation of Profitability

Let's start with a deceptively simple question: Where do profits come from? This might seem like a strange question to you. You're probably more used to questions like: What are our profits? What will they be next month? Next year? These are fine questions, but to answer them properly, you first have to understand where profits come from.

In the Introduction, I stated that profits are a piece of some larger economic pie. And the most fundamental of economic pies is the value created when a buyer and seller do a deal. To make this idea concrete, consider one of the simplest deals: a transaction at a yard sale. Although such a transaction might seem trivial compared to the transactions that drive most businesses, the principles behind it are not. *Profitability requires value creation*, and there is no value creation without deals.

Suppose that, at the yard sale, the homeowner, Mary, wants to sell a used, but well-functioning lawnmower to one of her neighbors, John. Many people have come to the sale, but only John has shown any interest in buying the mower. To understand how value will be created in this deal, we need to realize that both the buyer (John) and the seller (Mary) have a "walkaway" price. There are sufficiently low prices at which John would be willing to buy the lawnmower, as well as sufficiently high prices at which he would not. The walkaway price is the price that lies between these two ranges. In other words, if Mary offers a price below John's walkaway price, then John will buy. If Mary insists on a price above the walkaway price, then John will not buy—he will walk away. John's walkaway price has a standard name in economics: the buyer's **willingness to pay**, abbreviated **WTP**. The term "willingness to pay" is chosen to remind us that this is the highest price at which the buyer would be willing to pay for the good.

Next, we need to consider how John will feel if he buys the lawnmower at any price less than his WTP. For instance, suppose that his WTP for the lawnmower is $100, and he takes it home for only $40. He might say that he "paid $60 less than he would have" or that he "saved $60." The key point here is that this $60 in "savings" is the buyer's *profit* in this deal. While it may seem strange to use the term "profit" when referring to the buyer—after all, we usually think of a seller or a company making a profit—it's important to remember that *buyers make profits, too.* The buyer's WTP is, by definition, his valuation of the product. If he gets the product for any amount less than his WTP, this is a gain—or profit—for the buyer. Thus, a **buyer's profit** is defined as *the buyer's WTP minus what the buyer actually pays—that is, WTP minus p, where p is the price the buyer paid.* Using the numbers from this example, we have

Buyer profit = WTP − p = \$100 − \$40 = \$60

or, in other words, the \$60 "savings" mentioned above.

In this book, I will use two terms interchangeably: **value capture** and profits. The term "value capture" is useful because it reminds us that profits are nothing more than a piece of an economic pie, and that being profitable requires us to capture a piece of that pie. In the yard sale example, instead of saying that John made a profit of \$60, we could just as easily say that he *captured \$60 of value.*

Of course, there is another side to our lawnmower example—namely that of our seller, Mary, who parted with her lawnmower. There are sufficiently high prices at which she would be willing to sell the lawnmower and sufficiently low prices at which she would not. Once again, the walkaway price is the price between these two ranges of prices. If John offers a price above Mary's walkaway price, then Mary will sell. However, if John insists on a price below her walkaway price, Mary will not sell—she will walk away.

We generally use one of three terms to refer to the seller's walkaway price: **cost**, **opportunity cost**, or **economic cost**. "Economic cost" is the safest to use, as it means the same thing to everyone who knows the term. You'll find more formal definitions of both willingness-to-pay and economic cost in chapter 3, but for now, here are two equivalent ways to think about economic cost that have helped my students:

1. If you sold your product for less than your economic cost, your company would be worse off than if you had not sold the product.

2. Suppose that it is your job to negotiate the price at which to sell the product. At what price would you prefer to walk away from the negotiation rather than sell?

Returning to our homeowner, let's suppose that Mary's (economic) cost for the lawnmower is \$10. There could be any number of reasons for this: Maybe her brother-in-law had already offered her \$10 for the lawnmower. Or perhaps she had decided to keep the mower as a spare if she could not get at least \$10 for it. Whatever her reason, Mary will not sell the lawnmower for less than \$10. If, as above, we assume that the buyer and seller negotiate a price of $40, Mary will make a profit of $30. If we let the letter c denote the seller's economic cost, we can write

Seller's profit = price − cost = $p - c$ = $40 − $10 = $30

Now it is relatively easy to calculate the value created in this deal: You just add up each player's value capture. In this example the buyer captured $60, and the seller captured $30, so we know that the total value created must be $60 + $30, or $90. I will often refer to the total value created as the "pie," which is short for economic pie. But because we should be more formal in our equations, we will use TVC to denote the **total value created**. Using our abbreviations, we see that the pie is just the sum of each player's value capture:

TVC = WTP − p + p − c = WTP − c

Note that we could have computed the total value created without even worrying about what price the buyer and seller agreed upon. As long as the deal was done, $90 of value would have been created, where the $90 is based on a buyer WTP of $100, offset by a seller cost of $10.

This insight is not just a product of algebraic manipulation. It is a consequence of one of the central themes of this book. If there are profits to be had, there must be some economic pie that can be created and divided. Before you can ask if your company will be profitable, you need to know if the company will be part of some larger value creation. In our simple buyer–seller example, answering this question is straightforward: Does the buyer's WTP exceed the seller's cost? If yes, there is a pie (equal to WTP − c), and both players will have the opportunity to make money. If no, there will be no deal, and thus no profit.

When we move to more complicated business situations, calculating the total value created (the pie) will not be as easy, but the principle will remain the same: There will have to be a collection of buyers with willingnesses to pay that exceed the economic costs of providing the products they want. Moreover, when there are many different players, there is only one way to determine who might make money and how much: by considering, first, the total value created and, then, who actually contributes to the TVC. Chapter 2 will introduce how this works, but we'll preview the approach by revisiting our lawnmower example one last time.

In the lawnmower example, we know that there will be value creation if the buyer's WTP exceeds the seller's cost. Given our assumptions above, this was the case (TVC = $100 − $10 = $90). So now we ask how this pie will be divided. As mentioned in the Introduction, the answer to this question will typically depend on both competition and bargaining. Our simple example with just one buyer and one seller is the extreme case in which competition has no effect; each player's profit results solely from his or her negotiation skill. For concreteness, we assumed above that the players negotiated a price of $40. In theory, any price between $10 and $100 would have been possible. But whatever price the players agreed to, note that price was treated as a *consequence*—in this example, the consequence of bargaining.

In the next chapter, we'll consider examples in which prices are a consequence of competition *and* bargaining. You'll see how treating price as a consequence leads to a relatively simple way for understanding profitability in the complex world of business interactions. Rather than try to figure out what prices firms will set, whether buyers buy at those prices, whether firms adjust prices in response to buyer behavior, and so on, we will attack the problem from another direction. We'll first identify the total value that can be created—that is, the TVC—and then determine how that value should be divided among the players in a competitive environment. With an understanding of the effects of competition on the value players should capture, it then becomes relatively easy to know where prices are likely to end up. The next chapter starts to explain how this works.

2 Contributed Value and Unrestricted Competition

Value creation requires deals, but at what price will those deals be done? In this chapter, I begin to answer that question by looking at how important each player is to value creation. To do this, I will use examples based on industrial products. As we will discuss in chapter 3, determining a buyer's WTP for different products is often one of the most difficult judgments you will have to make. With an industrial product, though, the buyer's WTP is often based on a well-defined alternative with identifiable costs, and we will assume that this is the case in our example.

Suppose that a technology firm, which we'll call ProScan, is considering building a prototype of a new kind of medical scanner. Initially, the only customer for this scanner will be a medical products manufacturer, which we'll call MedCare. MedCare's management has calculated a willingness to pay of up to $50 million dollars for the scanner. This WTP is based on MedCare's potential net benefit from the scanner. In other words, MedCare would be indifferent between buying the scanner for $50 million dollars and not buying it. Additionally, we assume that ProScan's costs for producing the prototype scanner will total $25 million.

This situation is similar to that in our lawnmower example, so the initial analysis will be familiar. But before proceeding, let me go back to a term that I discussed briefly in the Introduction, one that will appear throughout the remainder of this book: a business *game*. There are two elements to a business game: the *players* in the game and the potential *value creation* of every possible deal. In the lawnmower game, there were only two players—John and Mary, the buyer and the seller. In the current example, we again have a two-player game. Only one deal is possible—namely MedCare doing business with ProScan—and we know from our lawnmower example that the value created in this deal is simply the WTP minus the cost. The pie is then $25 million:

TVC = $50M – $25M = $25M

If you are remembering the lawnmower example, you might guess that these two players should negotiate a price for the scanner between $25 and $50 million dollars— and you would be right. Let's consider some intuition behind why the negotiations could end up with any price in this range. First, note that both players are needed if any value is going to be created. Without MedCare, there is no buyer. With no buyer, there is no transaction. With no transaction, there is no value creation. Consequently, MedCare can argue that because it is essential to the value creation, it should get most of the value created in the deal. This implies that MedCare would pay a price close to ProScan's cost of $25 million.

The problem with this argument, though, is that ProScan can make a similar claim. Without ProScan, there is no seller. With no seller, there is no transaction. With no transaction, there is no value creation. Consequently, ProScan can argue that because it is essential to the value creation, *it* should get most of the value created in the deal. This implies that ProScan would receive a price close to MedCare's WTP of $50 million.

Contributed Value

These two arguments might seem contradictory, but, in fact, they are both correct. They use a concept that lies at the heart of competition: **contributed value**. A player's contributed value is simply the value that a player contributes to the economic pie. To determine a player's contributed value (ConV), you first calculate the total value created. Then you subtract the value created *without that player* from the TVC:

Player's contributed value (ConV) = TVC – *Value created without player*

Computing a player's contributed value is a thought experiment—that is, you ask yourself what would happen to the value creation if the player of interest were not in the game. Contributed value is a preliminary measure of a player's economic importance. You'll see, shortly, how contributed value is related to a player's ability to make a profit.

Returning to our example, the TVC was $25 million, so we have

ProScan's ConV = TVC – Value created without ProScan = $25M – 0 = $25M

and

MedCare's ConV = TVC – Value created without MedCare = $25M – 0 = $25M

Each player can reasonably claim that it deserves to capture most of the value because each contributes an amount equal to the whole pie. There is no reason why

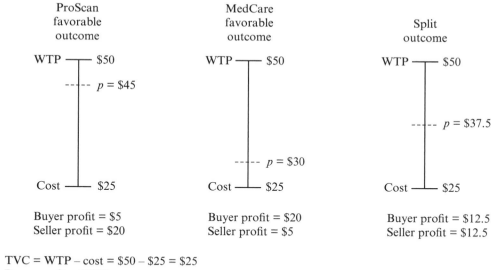

ProScan favorable outcome

MedCare favorable outcome

Split outcome

Buyer profit = $5
Seller profit = $20

Buyer profit = $20
Seller profit = $5

Buyer profit = $12.5
Seller profit = $12.5

TVC = WTP – cost = $50 – $25 = $25
Buyer profit = WTP – p
Seller (firm) profit = p – cost

Figure 2.1
Three possible outcomes of *Game 2.1*

one player's claim is any more legitimate than that of the other's, so, as noted earlier, almost any outcome is possible. Let's call this example *Game 2.1*, and we will use figure 2.1 to remind us of the range of possible outcomes. The figure depicts three representative outcomes: a ProScan-favorable outcome, a MedCare-favorable outcome, and a "split-the-difference" outcome. The gap between WTP and the price p depicts the buyer's profit, and the gap between p and *cost* depicts the seller's profit.

Introducing Competition to the Game

Let's introduce some competition by bringing another buyer into the game. This second buyer, which we'll call HealthCo, is another medical products manufacturer. Let's assume that it, too, is willing to pay up to $50 million for the prototype scanner. We now have a three-player game—*Game 2.2*—with one seller—ProScan—and two buyers—MedCare and HealthCo. Note that even though we have added another player, the pie is unchanged: there is still only one scanner, and so there will be only one transaction. Since both buyers have the same willingness to pay, there will be $25 million of value creation no matter who buys the scanner.

But even though the pie has not changed, the contributed value of each buyer has. Without MedCare, ProScan would sell to HealthCo, and $25 million would still be created. MedCare contributes no value. Without HealthCo, ProScan would sell to MedCare, and, again, $25 million would be created. HealthCo contributes no value. By contrast, without ProScan, there is no scanner to sell. ProScan contributes $25 million of value. We can summarize this as

MedCare ConV = TVC − Value created without MedCare = $25M − $25M = 0

Healthco ConV = TVC − Value created without HealthCo = $25M − $25M = 0

ProScan ConV = TVC − Value created without ProScan = $25M − 0 = $25M

The reasoning above suggests that ProScan should capture all the value. Let's look at the intuition for this reasoning. Because there are two buyers and only one scanner, one buyer will be left out. Remember that a buyer is indifferent between buying at its WTP—in this case, $50 million—and not buying. So either buyer would prefer to buy the scanner for any amount less than $50 million than to be left out. The seller, ProScan, knowing this, can go back and forth between the buyers until one agrees to pay a price close to $50 million. At that price the buyer captures virtually nothing—remember that the buyer's value capture is WTP minus price—and the seller makes a profit of $25 million.

Figure 2.2 below summarizes the situation. The price will be equal to the buyer's WTP, so the buyer will capture no value. The seller will capture all the value creation.

Recall that in our first game—with only one buyer—there was no competition, and either player could get some, none, or all of the value created. The outcome would depend solely on a negotiation between buyer and seller. In the second game, there is only one possible outcome: ProScan captures all the value. Bargaining played no role in the outcome; competition alone determined the outcome. In both games, our reasoning relied on an implicit assumption that I will call *unrestricted competition*. I'll describe it now and show how it is related to contributed value.

Unrestricted Competition

Games 2.1 and *2.2* illustrate the two extremes mentioned in the Introduction: competition perfectly determining profits and competition having no effect on profits. Despite these extremes, in both examples, the analysis shared the following property: *a player never captured more than its contributed value*. In *Game 2.1*, each player's contributed value equaled the pie, so, with any split of the pie, each player would get less than its

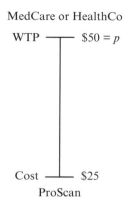

$$TVC = WTP - cost = \$25$$
MedCare ConV = 0; HealthCo ConV = 0. This implies p = WTP = $50.
ProScan ConV = $25
ProScan profit = p – cost = $25

Figure 2.2
Outcome of *Game 2.2*

contributed value. In *Game 2.2*, each player got exactly its contributed value. ProScan was the only player with positive contributed value and was the only player to make a profit.

In hindsight, it shouldn't seem surprising that no player captured more than it contributed. After all, why should players in a game take away more than they contribute? The answer is that they shouldn't. If a player, or a group of players, never captures more than it contributes, we say that competition is *unrestricted*. Competition is unrestricted if *no player, or group of players, captures more than it contributes, and all the players, collectively, capture what they contribute.*

I use the term "unrestricted" because with this form of competition, there are no restrictions on the players' ability to find and make jointly profitable deals. (In the appendix to chapter 6, you'll see that this model of competition lies at the heart of supply and demand reasoning.) In fact, this notion of "unrestricted" provides an alternative way to define unrestricted competition. *If competition is unrestricted, no jointly profitable deal between any group of players is left unexecuted.* That is, when competition is unrestricted, there is never a better deal that a player or group of players could have done on their own. For this reason, we sometimes describe unrestricted competition as the requirement that "no good deal goes undone." But remember, this is equivalent to saying that no player captures more than it contributes, and that no group of players capture more than they contribute, collectively.

I've already discussed how the outcome in *Game 2.2* is consistent with no player capturing more than its contributed value. Let's look at the same game from the no-good-deal-goes-undone perspective. Suppose that one of the buyers, say MedCare, were going to buy the scanner for only $40 million. This would give MedCare a profit of $10 million, which exceeds its contributed value of zero. If this were to happen, competition would not be unrestricted, and there should be a jointly favorable deal for some group of players. Let's find that deal. First, let's summarize the proposed scenario:

Proposed scenario: MedCare buys at price of $40M

MedCare's profit = WTP $- p =$ $50M $-$ $40M $=$ $10M

HealthCo's profit = 0 (They are left out of the deal.)

ProScan's profit = $p -$ cost = $40M $-$ $25M $=$ $15M

HealthCo gets nothing, so, if it can buy the scanner at any price less than its WTP, it will be better off. And if ProScan can sell for more than the proposed price of $40 million, it will be better off as well. Here is the better deal that is left undone: HealthCo buying from ProScan at a price between $40 million and $50 million.

For concreteness, let's suppose that HealthCo tries to buy at $45 million. Then, we have the following better deal for HealthCo and ProScan:

"Better" deal: HealthCo buys at price of $45M

MedCare's profit = 0 (they are left out of the deal)

HealthCo's profit = WTP $- p =$ $50M $-$ $45M $=$ $5M (better than 0!)

ProScan's profit = $p -$ cost = $45M $-$ $25M $=$ $20M (better that $15M!)

But now MedCare captures no value. By similar reasoning, MedCare and ProScan both prefer an "even better" deal in which MedCare buys at a price between $45 and $50 million, say $47.5 million. By repeating this sort of story, you can see how the assumption of "no good deal goes undone" will lead to a price close to $50 million.

I have just given you a story that closely follows the mathematics used in this chapter's appendix. But at this point, you might want to come up with your own intuition for this example. For instance, you could think of this situation as the seller playing the buyers off against each other, as I did when I first introduced *Game 2.2*. Or you could think of this as a price war. Whatever intuition you choose, it is true that unrestricted competition assumes a particularly aggressive form of competition. When we get to strategy applications, this assumption will be useful. If you can make an argument for why you should make money under the most competitively extreme situations, then you can make an argument for making money in any situation.

Competition and Bargaining: The Pessimistic Base Case

Game 2.2 reflects a situation that any company would like to be in: excess demand. With excess demand, buyers must compete for a firm's product. (In part III of this book, we'll look at the effects of excess demand in detail.) But in many business situations, it feels as if the situation is reversed: a firm must compete for its buyers. In fact, this is often the implicit assumption in a lot of strategy advice. For instance, whenever someone claims that to be profitable, you have to be different from the competition, they are implicitly assuming that firms must compete for buyers. This is actually a useful base case for a strategic analysis, for if you are profitable when there is an excess of products chasing a limited number of buyers, then you are profitable when competition is working against you. So let's preview how to be profitable when you are competing for a limited number of buyers.

In *Game 2.3* we return to a situation in which MedCare is the only buyer, and there is a competitor for ProScan, which we'll call TechScan. We'll assume that, just like its competitor, TechScan incurs costs of $25 million to produce its scanner, and that the only buyer, MedCare, is willing to pay as much as $50 million for it. Figure 2.3 depicts the game. Now that we have more than one firm, it will be useful to give the stick figures a name. We call them **value gaps**. *A firm's value gap is the difference between the customer's WTP for the firm's product and the firm's economic cost for providing the product.* In other words, it is the value that a firm can create with a customer. Because each value gap represents a different firm, value gaps provide a visual way to compare firms. For instance, in figure 2.3, it is easy to see that the buyer, MedCare, has the same willingness to pay for each seller's product. Additionally, it is easy to see that the two firms have the same costs.

As in the previous game, the addition of another player does not change the total value created. There are now two firms, but because there is only one buyer in the game, only one deal can be made. Thus, the total value created remains at $25 million. If we do a thought experiment to assess contributed values, we see that if ProScan drops out of the game, the pie remains the same because TechScan will step in to make the sale. Thus, ProScan contributes no value. The same will be true if TechScan drops out—TechScan contributes no value. Note that when calculating each players's ConV, it

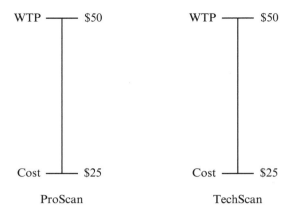

TVC = WTP – cost = $25
MedCare ConV = $25
ProScan ConV = 0; TechScan ConV = 0. This implies p = cost = $25.
MedCare profit = WTP – p = $25

Figure 2.3
Game 2.3

doesn't matter who was going to buy from whom before the thought experiment; when we remove any player to determine its ConV, we assume that the remaining players will make the best deal possible.

Finally, without MedCare, there is no buyer, and hence no deal. MedCare's ConV is then the whole pie, namely $25 million. If competition is unrestricted, we know what should happen: ProScan and TechScan contribute nothing and so will make nothing; MedCare will capture the whole pie. Translating this into a price, we have $25 million. There are two ways to arrive at this price.

1. Because ProScan and TechScan capture nothing, for whichever company sells to MedCare, it must be the case that p – *cost* = 0. Since cost equals $25 million, the price, p, must be $25 million.

2. Because MedCare captures $25 million, it must be that WTP – p = $25 million. Since MedCare's WTP is $50 million, the price, p, must be $25 million.

In *Game 2.3* profits are determined solely by competition, just as in *Game 2.2*. Unlike *Game 2.2*, though, competition gives all the profit to the buyer. The final two games in this chapter will involve situations in which both bargaining and competition determine profitability.

Competition and Bargaining: A Preview of Being Better

Game 2.4 is the same as *Game 2.3* but with one difference: TechScan's costs are now lower. Instead of $25 million, they are $20 million. For our purposes, the reason that they are lower is not so important. (You could imagine, say, that TechScan's production process has lower labor costs or uses raw materials more efficiently.) Figure 2.4 depicts the game. As in figure 2.3, there is one value gap for each company.

TechScan's lower cost produces several important changes in this game. First, note that the pie has increased by $5 million, to $30 million (WTP − *cost* = $50 million − $20 million). With unrestricted competition, the TVC is always calculated to yield the largest *possible* value creation in the game, which in this case is the difference between MedCare's WTP and TechScan's cost. Next, note that TechScan is now contributing value in this game. Value can be created without TechScan, but not as much— MedCare buying from ProScan creates $25 million, not $30 million. Consequently, TechScan contributes $5 million. Intuitively, TechScan contributes value because it has lower costs.

Another important point is that TechScan is not guaranteed to get $5 million. It could, in fact, get zero. To see why, note that MedCare's ConV is $30—the whole pie. If

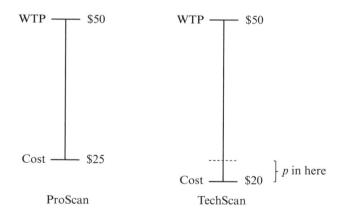

$$TVC = WTP - cost = \$30$$
MedCare ConV = $30
ProScan ConV = 0
TechScan ConV = $5. This implies $p - cost$ can be up to $5, with p up to $25.

Figure 2.4
Game 2.4

MedCare captures all of its contributed value, this leaves nothing for TechScan. But Medcare is guaranteed to capture some value. Suppose that TechScan captures all of its contributed value of $5 million. Because $30 million is created, this must leave $25 million for MedCare. As a result, we know that MedCare could get between $25 million and $30 million, leaving TechScan with between zero and $5 million. So how much will each player actually get? We don't know—MedCare and TechScan will negotiate over this $5 million.

Let's summarize the situation:

- Competition between ProScan and TechScan guarantees that Medcare captures at least $25 million of value.
- TechScan's contributed value is $5 million due to being $5 million "better" than its competitor (its costs are $5 million lower than ProScan's).
- But TechScan has to bargain with MedCare to get this $5 million.

Translating between Prices and Value Capture

Our final step in this example is to see what our conclusions about value capture imply for the price that MedCare will pay TechScan. We will do this formulaically, but first, to gain some intuition, let's consider a hypothetical pricing war. ProScan might begin by offering its scanner for $45 million, and TechScan might counter by offering it for $40 million. Sooner or later, TechScan will offer its scanner for $25 million, a price below which ProScan cannot go without selling at a loss. At this point, the competition is over. MedCare is *guaranteed* a price no higher than $25 million, and TechScan *might* receive a price of $25 million. However, although the competition is over, the game is not. MedCare tells TechScan that it wants to pay only $20 million for the scanner. TechScan tells MedCare that it is not interested in selling for less than $25 million. The negotiation has begun. Where it ends up, only TechScan and MedCare can determine.

With the intuition of our story as background, let's formally connect the value-capture possibilities to price. If MedCare captures all of its contributed value of $30 million, then it must be that WTP $- p = \$30$ million. Since MedCare's WTP is $50 million, the price, p, must be at least $20 million. If TechScan captures all of its contributed value of $5 million, it must be the case that $p - cost = \$5$ million. Since TechScan's cost equals $20 million, the price, p, must be, at most, $25 million. We can conclude that the price will be between $20 million and $25 million, as depicted in figure 2.4. In short:

Competition guarantees MedCare a profit of at least $25 million.

Bargaining between MedCare and TechScan will determine how an additional $5 million in profits will be split.

Prices as a Consequence—Revisited

At this point, you might ask: Why doesn't TechScan just set a price of $25 million? The answer, of course, is that MedCare might simply respond by demanding that TechScan accept a price of $20 million. If you adopt the mindset of a typical American consumer, you expect stores to have posted prices, and you know that it is rare to be able to negotiate to pay anything other than the posted price. But, in reality, nonnegotiable posted prices are the exception. Almost all transactions between businesses are negotiated, and in many parts of the world even the prices of consumer products are negotiated. In the United States, for example, the prices of some products—such as cars and high-end audio equipment—are negotiable. So if you want to be sure that a firm will make a profit, you cannot rely on the firm negotiating successfully. Instead, you have to understand how much of a firm's profits will be guaranteed by competition, and how much will be due to successful—or perhaps not so successful—bargaining.

Competition and Bargaining: Another Preview of Being Better

The analysis of our final game in this chapter will be very similar to that of the previous game. Instead of giving one company a cost advantage, though, we will give the other company a WTP advantage. We will sometimes call a WTP advantage a *preference advantage*. If a company has a WTP advantage over another company, it means that the customer is willing to pay more for its product than for the other company's product. Quite simply, the customer prefers the first company's product and is willing to pay more for it. In figure 2.5, ProScan has a WTP advantage over TechScan.

As before, the buyer's reason for having a higher WTP for ProScan's scanner is not our main concern here. Maybe ProScan's scanner is more reliable, resulting in lower maintenance costs. Or maybe it scans more quickly, increasing the number of scans its machine can perform per day. Whatever the reason, MedCare's higher WTP for ProScan's product gives ProScan a contributed value of $5 million. MedCare still has a contributed value of $30 million, so our analysis is almost the same as before. MedCare will be guaranteed $25 million of value capture. MedCare and ProScan will negotiate over the remaining $5 million. When we describe this in terms of price, we just have to remember that ProScan's costs are $25 million. The negotiation over the $5 million will

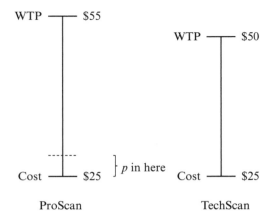

TVC = WTP − cost = $30
MedCare ConV = $30
ProScan ConV = $5. This implies *p* − cost can be up to $5, with *p* up to $30.
TechScan ConV = 0

Figure 2.5
Game 2.5

be a negotiation of a price between $25 million and $30 million, as shown in figure 2.5. Thus,

Competition guarantees a profit of at least $25 million to Medcare.

Bargaining between Medcare and ProScan will determine how an additional $5 million in profits will be split.

In both *Games 2.4* and *2.5*, the profitable firm was the firm with the largest value gap: the difference between the customer's WTP for the firm's product and the firm's economic cost for providing the product. In part II, we will see how having the largest value gap is essential to being profitable when a firm has to compete for customers. From *Games 2.4* and *2.5*, you might suspect that one key to profitability is to have either lower costs (*Game 2.4*) or a better product (*Game 2.5*). In fact, many business schools still teach that a firm *must* have either a low cost or differentiated—that is, better product—strategy. As mentioned in the Introduction, you will see that this is, at best, limited and, at worst, simply incorrect.

We have been talking about willingness to pay and economic cost without properly defining these terms, so we will discuss them in more depth in chapter 3. We'll focus especially on WTP, as the notion of willingness to pay is not natural for many people.

We usually are well aware of what we pay for things, but we are not always so aware of the most we would pay if we had to.

A Note on Restricted Competition

Throughout this book, we will use unrestricted competition as a baseline assumption. As I noted earlier in this chapter, this assumes that all players are aggressively competitive. But what if the players are not competing aggressively? In other words, what will happen if competition is not unrestricted? As noted in the Introduction, there is no general theory for situations in which competition is restricted. But given a game, we can say what outcomes would imply that competition is restricted. To demonstrate, we'll revisit *Games 2.3*, *2.4*, and *2.5*.

In *Game 2.3*, neither firm makes any money under unrestricted competition. So if either ProScan or TechScan (or both) made a profit, then we would know that competition was not unrestricted. Without further information, though, we wouldn't know why it was unrestricted. We would have to do more research. We might find, for instance, that ProScan and TechScan were colluding. Or perhaps TechScan decided not to compete for the customer for some reason. Or the customer might not have wanted to compete aggressively and, thus, accepted an offer from one firm without consulting the other. Whatever the reason, all we know for sure is that profits for either ProScan or TechScan imply that competition is restricted. Similarly, in *Games 2.4* and *2.5*, ProScan could capture up to $5 million and TechScan could not make any profit. So, if ProScan captured more than $5 million, or if TechScan made any profit, competition would be restricted.

Now it is also true, as a matter of logic, that outcomes consistent with unrestricted competition don't *necessarily* mean that competition is unrestricted. But because unrestricted competition is a conservative assumption from the perspective of firm profitability, we'll assume that it holds unless either our knowledge of the specific context tells us to relax it or the current profitability of some of the players contradicts it.

Three Conceptual Points to Remember

• Competition alone does not typically determine profits—there is usually some residual bargaining.
• Think of prices in the marketplace as a consequence of both competition and bargaining.
• If competition is unrestricted, you must contribute value to be profitable.

Appendix: The Mathematics of Unrestricted Competition

To define unrestricted competition, one first models the context of interest as a game in characteristic function form (also called a "cooperative" game). A game in characteristic function is defined by two entities: a *player set* and a *characteristic function*. The player set is almost self-explanatory; it is the collection of players in the context of interest. In *Game 2.5*, the player set contained MedCare, ProScan, and TechScan. Using N to denote the player set, we would write

$N = \{$MedCare, ProScan, TechScan$\}$

A *characteristic function* specifies the value that can be created by any possible group of players. With three players, there are eight possible groups (or *subsets*) of players. We list them in table 2.1, along with the value that each group can create.

The left column lists all the combinations of players. The right column lists how much value the given group of players can create together. At the top of each column, I've put the standard notation. An unspecified subset of the player set N is usually depicted with an S, and the value created by a subset S of the players is depicted by $v(S)$. For instance, if $S = \{$MedCare, ProScan$\}$, then

$v(S) = v(\{$MedCare, ProScan$\}) = \$30M$

If you revisit *Game 2.5*, you should be able to make sense of table 2.1. No value is created by a player acting on its own in this game, so $v(S) = 0$ when S is a group with just one player. Without a buyer, no value is created, so we must also have $v(\{$ProScan, TechScan$\}) = 0$. As we argued earlier, $v(\{$MedCare, TechScan$\}) = \$25M$. Finally, note that

$v(\{$MedCare, ProScan$\}) = v(\{$MedCare, ProScan, TechScan$\}) = \$30M$

Table 2.1

S	$v(S)$
{} (the group with no players)	0
{MedCare}	0
{ProScan}	0
{TechScan}	0
{MedCare, ProScan}	$30M
{MedCare, TechScan}	$25M
{ProScan, TechScan}	0
{MedCare, ProScan, TechScan}	$30M

Because MedCare is interested in buying only one scanner, TechScan adds nothing to the possible value creation. In fact, I've already argued that TechScan contributes zero value. Let's use the notation to show this again.

When computing the contributed value of a player, we usually write $v(N\setminus\{player\})$ to denote the value that can be created without the player in question. The expression $N\setminus\{player\}$ is an abbreviation for "everybody in the game except the player." Thus, to compute TechScan's contributed value, we have

$v(N) - v(N\setminus\{TechScan\})$
$\qquad = v(\{MedCare, ProScan, TechScan\}) - v(\{MedCare, ProScan\})$
$\qquad = \$30M - \$30M = 0$

which is just what we found earlier.

Before defining unrestricted competition, I'll introduce one more piece of notation to represent a player's profit—that is, its value capture. For any group (or set) of players S, we let $x(S)$ denote the sum of the profits for the players in the group—that is, the value captured by the players in set S. For instance, the individual profits of MedCare, ProScan, and TechScan would be represented by $x(\{MedCare\})$, $x(\{ProScan\})$, and $x(\{TechScan\})$, respectively. As another example, if $S = \{MedCare, ProScan\}$, we would write

$x(S) = x(\{MedCare, ProScan\}) = x(\{MedCare\}) + x(\{ProScan\})$

Unrestricted Competition

We can now define unrestricted competition. Competition is unrestricted if the players' profits satisfy two conditions: the *competitive condition* and the *feasibility condition*. (In the game theory literature, these two conditions describe the *core* of a game in characteristic function form.)

The *competitive* condition: For any possible subset of players S (including the set of all players N), $x(S) \geq v(S)$.

In words, the sum of the profits for a group of players must be as least as large as the value the group can create on its own. This is the "no good deal goes undone" condition. If it were the case that $x(S) < v(S)$, then the players in S would be "leaving money on the table." They would do better by acting on their own and splitting $v(S)$ among themselves. And we know that a split would exist that makes them all better off because $v(S) > x(S)$. Also, note that the competitive condition requires one to check whether $x(S) \geq v(S)$ for every possible subset of players. For *Game 2.5* this means that we'll have to check seven equations, one for each line of table 2.1.

The *feasibility* condition: $x(N) \le v(N)$.

In words, this condition merely says that you can't divide up more than you have: player profits cannot total more than the value that all the players together can create. This is called a feasibility condition because, if it did not hold, you'd be able to divide a pie into pieces that would add up to something bigger than the original pie.

Competition Implies Efficiency

Note that the competitive condition, when applied to the set of all players N, tells us that $x(N) \ge v(N)$. When we combine this with the feasibility condition, we have $x(N) = v(N)$. In words, I have just shown that unrestricted competition implies that the players will create and capture the greatest possible value, namely $v(N)$. Thus, with unrestricted competition, the total value created (TVC) will always be equal to $v(N)$. Because the largest amount of value will be created, we say that the outcome will be efficient. Thus, with unrestricted competition, competition implies efficiency.

Returning to *Game 2.5*, we can see how these conditions yield the same results as our verbal analysis. Consider the following four equations.

$$x(\{\text{MedCare, ProScan, TechScan}\}) \le v(N) = 30 \tag{1}$$

$$x(\{\text{MedCare, ProScan, TechScan}\}) \ge v(N) = 30 \tag{2}$$

$$x(\{\text{MedCare, ProScan}\}) \ge v(\{\text{MedCare, ProScan}\}) = 30 \tag{3}$$

$$x(\{\text{MedCare, TechScan}\}) \ge v(\{\text{MedCare, TechScan}\}) = 25 \tag{4}$$

Equation (1) is the feasibility condition, and equations (2), (3), and (4) are three of the seven equations that must be true for the competitive condition to hold. (Because $v(S) = 0$ in the other four equations, they won't affect our analysis.) Equations (1) and (2) imply that

$$x(\{\text{MedCare, ProScan, TechScan}\}) = 30$$

(This demonstrates the fact noted just above: with unrestricted competition, the total value created (TVC) will always be equal to $v(N)$.)

Combining this fact with equation (3), we have $x(\{\text{TechScan}\}) = 0$: TechScan makes zero profit. Bringing in equation (4), we must then have $x(\{\text{MedCare}\}) \ge 25$. MedCare captures at least 25. From equations (1) and (2) again, it follows that $x(\{\text{ProScan}\}) \le 5$. ProScan makes, at most, 5. This is the same result as before. We summarize the results

Table 2.2

S	x(S)	v(S)
{}	0	0
{MedCare}	$55M − p	0
{ProScan}	p − $25M	0
{TechScan}	0	0
{MedCare, ProScan}	$30M	$30M
{MedCare, TechScan}	$55M − p	$25M
{ProScan, TechScan}	p − $25M	0
{MedCare, ProScan, TechScan}	$30M	$30M

in table 2.2. The price p must be between $25 million and $30 million. Note that if the price were greater than $30 million, we would have

$x(\{MedCare, TechScan\}) < v(\{MedCare, TechScan\})$

and MedCare and TechScan would be "leaving money on the table."

Unrestricted Competition: The Contributed Value Perspective

In this chapter, I first introduced unrestricted competition in terms of contributed values. I said that *competition is unrestricted if no player, or group of players, captures more than it contributes, and all the players, collectively, capture what they contribute.* I'll end this appendix by showing that these two conditions are equivalent to the competitive and feasibility conditions.

First, the condition that all the players, collectively, capture what they contribute, just says that the players, collectively, capture all the possible value. We can even see this by translating the words into an equation:

$x(N) = v(N) − v(N \backslash N) = v(N)$

(The term $v(N \backslash N)$ might seem a bit awkward. The expression $N \backslash N$ is the empty set. In words, all the players in N without the players in N leaves no players. Thus the value created by no players must be zero—$v(N \backslash N) = v(\{\}) = 0$.)

Next, the condition that no player, or group of players, capture more than they contribute, means that for any possible subset of players S (including the set of all players N),

$x(S) \leq v(N) − v(N \backslash S)$

Now, the first condition gave us that $x(N) = v(N) - v(N \backslash N) = v(N)$, so the equation above becomes

$x(S) \leq x(N) - v(N \backslash S)$

Because $x(N \backslash S) = x(N) - x(S)$, the equation above becomes

$x(N \backslash S) \geq v(N \backslash S)$

This is just the competitive condition for the players in $N \backslash S$. In fact, I exploited this relationship when I first argued that players should not capture more than they contribute. Recall that if they did capture more than they contributed, the other players would prefer to do a deal on their own. Thus, if a group of players S were to capture more than they contribute, then the group of players $N \backslash S$ would be able to find a better deal for themselves.

3   Willingness to Pay and Economic Cost

This book began with a deal that might seem trivial from a business perspective—a yard sale transaction—but conceptually it is as important as any deal. Such transactions demonstrate value creation, and value creation is the building block for profitability—without a pie, no one gets a slice of pie—that is, profit. In the yard sale deal, the value created was simply the buyer's willingness to pay minus the seller's economic cost. If value creation is the building block of profitability, then these two concepts—buyer willingness to pay and seller economic cost—make up that block. Thus, you need to understand how to compute them and some of their implications. We do both in this chapter, starting with two implications of willingness to pay that are often overlooked.

WTP: The Benchmark for Buyer Profit

In our original lawnmower example, a buyer's willingness to pay was defined as the most the buyer would pay before preferring to walk away from the deal. This should seem reasonable. For any good you might want to buy, there clearly are prices sufficiently high that you would say "no thanks" to the seller. But once you agree that you have a willingness to pay for a product, you have established your benchmark for buyer profit. If you end up paying anything less than your WTP, you have captured value—if you pay a price p, WTP $-\ p$ is your profit. Alternatively, having made the purchase, you are better off by the amount WTP $-\ p$ than if you had not purchased. The proof of this assertion is straightforward: your WTP is, by definition, the most you will pay; if you pay less than this amount, you are better off—you've made a profit.

WTP: The Benchmark May Be Subjective

Another implication of willingness to pay is that value creation may be subjective. Remember, the total value created will be based on a calculation like WTP – c. The willingness to pay is a *buyer*'s willingness to pay—not what someone else is willing to pay or what you might think the buyer *should* be willing to pay. *It is the buyer's subjective calculation of what he is willing to pay.* This is not so surprising to marketing experts, who typically understand that the customer's perspective is the one that matters. For the rest of us, though, it is very easy to fall into the trap of having an opinion about what a buyer should be willing to pay, especially when we know very little about what the buyer's WTP might be. In these situations, we have to walk a fine line between making a judgment about what we *think* it is, without injecting our opinion about what it *should* be. This requires the classic skill of viewing the world from someone else's perspective, a skill that is notoriously difficult to master.

Calculating WTP

To build some intuition for these two implications—buyer profit and the subjectivity of WTP—it is useful to calculate the willingness to pay for an industrial product that has well-defined alternatives. Let's return to the product in our chapter 2 games: a medical scanner.

In the last chapter, we started with a WTP of $50 million for ProScan's scanner. Consider a situation in which this is based on a calculation with almost no subjectivity. Suppose that the buyer, say MedCare, was currently spending $2,800,000 per year to provide scanning to all its patients. Further suppose that this $2,800,000 was based on renting four scanners at $500,000 per year each, plus technician and maintenance labor costs of $800,000 per year. Now suppose that ProScan's new scanner has enough capacity to replace all four existing machines. In addition, with the reduction in the number of machines needed, suppose that the technician and maintenance costs are reduced to just $300,000 per year. Then, MedCare views the purchase decision as follows:

Status quo alternative: Keep paying $2,800,000 per year

or

Purchase scanner at price p: Pay p now, and pay $300,000 per year

The buyer's willingness to pay is defined as the price, p, at which it is indifferent between these two choices. Therefore, to calculate the WTP, we need to determine the price at which each option provides the same value to the buyer. (Mathematically, this is equivalent to solving the following equation for p: $-\$2,800,000/\text{year} = -\$p - \$300,000/\text{year}$.)

When we compare the two choices, we see that buying the new scanner will save MedCare $2,500,000 per year. At this point, MedCare must determine how much it values a savings of $2,500,000 per year over the lifetime of the scanner. This is a standard financial calculation, so let's say that MedCare's chief financial officer says that a $2,500,000 per year savings should be treated as equivalent to a onetime savings today of $50 million. With this number in hand, MedCare would be indifferent between the status quo and buying the new scanner for $50 million. Consequently, $50 million is MedCare's WTP for the scanner. (See this chapter's appendix for a decision tree analysis of this calculation.)

More important, though, if MedCare purchases the scanner for less than $50 million, it will be financially better off. Its financial situation will, in fact, improve by WTP $- p$—that is, $50M $- p$. It may not be easy to see this profit in the buyer's financial statements because this value capture occurs over the lifetime of the scanner. But if MedCare's accounting system isolates scanning costs in its income statement, these costs will be lower than if it had stayed with the status quo option. If you add up the reduction in scanning costs over the lifetime of the scanner and adjust these cost differences for the fact that they occur over time, you will get a total equal to the buyer's profit—namely WTP $- p$.

Fixed Outside Option

There is one assumption in this example that I want to highlight for future reference. In calculating the buyer's WTP, we assumed that the costs associated with the status quo alternative were fixed. In particular, we assumed that the rental company providing the four scanners would *not* offer a lower rental price if it thought that it would lose MedCare's business. In other words, we treated the status quo costs like a *fixed* outside option—the outside option would remain unchanged no matter what happened with the competition and bargaining over the price of ProScan's scanner. In the context of our example, this might not seem like a dramatic assumption, but, in fact, it is essential. Consider the following story: Company A is interested in entering a market with a product priced at $7.99. Company B is already in the market with a similar, possibly better, product priced at $8.99. Company A is sure that customers will pay $7.99 for its product. But what if Company B drops its price to $8.49? Will customers still buy from Company A? To answer this sort of question, we need to know a buyer's WTP for both

Company A's and Company B's product. And we cannot calculate a buyer's WTP for Company A by assuming that buying from Company B at $8.99 is the outside option. Why not? Because Company B might change its price if Company A were to enter the market.

To get around this problem, you simply have to base the WTP calculation on an outside option *that won't react.* Later, in part IV, we will talk about which players are "in the game" and which players are "out of the game." In *Games 2.4* and *2.5*, the players "in the game" were ProScan, TechScan, and MedCare. Players "out of the game" included the company renting the existing scanners and the technicians operating the scanners.

Determining who is in versus who is out of the game will be another of the key judgments you will have to make. In part IV, I will give you some guidelines to help you make this judgment, but for now, you can think of players in the game as your customers, both existing and potential, and any business that might actively compete with you.

Returning to WTP calculations, the key point to remember is that WTP acts as a kind of frame of reference for analyzing your business interactions. Thus, a buyer's WTP must be based on an option outside of the game. In our example above, because we assumed that the scanner rental company would not react to what happened in our game, we did not include it as a player in the game. Consequently, we could base our WTP calculation on the rental costs.

Subjectivity in a WTP

Let's now make MedCare's WTP more subjective. Let's start with the calculation we have so far: based on its status quo scanning costs, MedCare has a WTP of $50 million for either ProScan's or TechScan's scanner. But now suppose that MedCare believes that ProScan has a more innovative reputation in the field and that by buying its product, MedCare will gain public relations value in its ongoing branding campaign—designed to position MedCare as the preeminent company in its business. For concreteness, suppose that MedCare's management considers this public relations benefit equivalent to the benefit from a $5 million advertising campaign. MedCare's WTP for ProScan's product would now be $55 million. Note that ProScan does not have to believe in the public relations benefit—nor do we. We are talking about *MedCare's* WTP, so all that matters is *MedCare's* (subjective) belief about the public relations benefit.

WTP for a Consumer Product

An industrial product with a well-defined alternative provides a clear example for calculating willingness to pay. And as I showed above, even if there is a subjective element to the calculation, there still is some basis for determining the buyer's WTP. But what if there isn't a well-defined alternative? For instance, how do we compute the willingness to pay for a consumer product, particularly a discretionary product? The standard procedure doesn't help much:

Status quo alternative: Don't buy the product

or

Purchase product at price p: Get product, have p fewer dollars

Making these two choices equivalent tells us to find the price p at which the buyer is indifferent between buying and not buying. But this is just the definition of WTP.

Assessing a consumer's willingness to pay for products like these is one of the toughest tasks in business. It is complicated by at least two factors: (1) people may not know what they want, and (2) even if they do, their willingness-to-pay for a product can change based on the context.

Fortunately, there is a whole discipline devoted to this task—marketing. With no well-defined alternatives to establish a willingness to pay, you will have to rely on your own judgment and your marketing experts' judgment to assess customer WTP for your products. In the Introduction, I explained that I would rely on you, the reader, to provide key judgments. Assessing a customer's willingness to pay is one of the most important—and difficult—judgments you will have to make.

Inferring Bounds on WTP: Revealed Preference

Although it can be very difficult to assess a buyer's willingness to pay, it is possible to obtain some information about buyers' WTP from their behavior. Economists call this "revealed preference." The idea is that people reveal information about their preference—that is, their WTP—by what they choose and don't choose to buy at certain prices.

To see how this works, keep two things in mind. First, a buyer's profit is WTP $- p$. Second, a buyer prefers more profit to less profit. Using these two facts, we will answer two questions:

1. If a buyer is paying a price premium for your product, that is, if a buyer is paying more for your product than for a competitor's product, what do we know about his WTP?

2. If a buyer is buying your product at a discount, that is, if a buyer is paying less for your product than for a competitor's product, what do we know about his WTP?

The answers to these questions are easy to state:

1. If a buyer is paying a price premium for your product, *you have a WTP advantage at least as large as the premium.*

2. If a buyer is buying your product at a discount, *your WTP disadvantage is no bigger than the discount.*

To justify these answers, we need a little notation. Let's talk about a company A and a company B. Company A will be the company that the buyer purchases from, and company B will be some competitor. Rather than continually writing "willingness to pay for company A's product," I'll simply write WTP(A). The notation for the price paid to company A will be $p(A)$. For company B, the respective terms will be WTP(B) and $p(B)$.

Price Premium: You Have a WTP Advantage at Least as Big as the Premium

Because the customer is buying from company A, his buyer profit is WTP(A) – $p(A)$. Because a buyer prefers more profit to less, it must be the case that he gets more profit buying from company A than from company B. Thus, it must be the case that

WTP(A) – $p(A)$ ≥ WTP(B) – $p(B)$

In words, the buyer captures more value buying from company A than from company B when the prices are $p(A)$ and $p(B)$, respectively.

Rearranging terms, this is the same as

WTP(A) – WTP(B) ≥ $p(A)$ – $p(B)$

The difference in prices—namely, $p(A)$ – $p(B)$—is the price premium your company is receiving. In words, *if your company is receiving a price premium over a competitor, your willingness-to-pay (or preference) advantage is at least as big as the price premium.* For instance, if your customers are paying $2.00 more for your product than for a competitor's product, their WTP for your product is at least $2.00 more than their WTP for your competitor's product. In fact, your WTP advantage over your competitor could be much greater than $2.00, but we don't know that for sure. All we know is that it is at least $2.00.

Price Discount: Your WTP Disadvantage Is No Bigger Than the Discount

We still have the buyer purchasing from company A, so it must still be the case that

$$WTP(A) - p(A) \geq WTP(B) - p(B)$$

But now the customer is buying at a discount, so $p(A)$ is less than $p(B)$. Thus we need to rearrange our terms differently:

$$p(B) - p(A) \geq WTP(B) - WTP(A)$$

In words, if your company is providing a price discount relative to a competitor, your willingness-to-pay (or preference) disadvantage is no bigger than the discount. For instance, if your customers are paying $2.00 less for your product than for a competitor's product, their WTP for your product is, at worst, $2.00 less than the WTP for your competitor's product. Your WTP disadvantage could be much less than $2.00. You could even have a WTP advantage. But we don't know. All we know for sure is that, at worst, the WTP for company A's product is only $2.00 less than the WTP for company B's product.

Inferring Bounds on Premiums and Discounts

These first two questions look at what we can deduce about customers' WTP from what they are actually buying. They address the question: What do prices imply about willingness to pay? The next two questions explore the reverse implications. Given buyers' willingnesses to pay, what can we deduce about where prices should end up? This question matters because it will help you understand what it will take to "win the customer," a topic we address in part II.

3. If a buyer has a higher WTP for a company's product, what is the maximum premium price that the company can get?
4. If a buyer has a lower WTP for a company's product, what is the minimum discount that the company must offer?

The next two sections answer these two questions.

A Price Premium Can Be No Larger Than a WTP Advantage

As before, we have the customer buying from company A. So, again, we have

$$WTP(A) - p(A) \geq WTP(B) - p(B)$$

Since we're considering the case in which the buyer has a higher WTP for company A's product than for company B's product, we have the same rearrangement as in our answer to question 1:

$$WTP(A) - WTP(B) \geq p(A) - p(B)$$

Although the expression is the same as in question 1, remember that now we are starting with WTP and asking what we know about prices. In words, then, this expression can be interpreted as follows: If the customer has a higher WTP for company A's than for company B's product, company A can have a higher price than company B—that is, a price premium—and still make the sale—that is, win the customer. *The price premium can be as large as the size of the WTP advantage—[WTP(A) − WTP(B)]—but no larger.* So, if company A's product has a WTP advantage of $4.00 over company B's, then a buyer will pay up to $4.00 more for company A's product.

A Price Discount Must Be at Least as Large as a WTP Disadvantage

As in the other cases, we start with

$$WTP(A) - p(A) \geq WTP(B) - p(B)$$

Now we consider the case in which the buyer has a lower WTP for company A's product than for company B's, so we have the same rearrangement as in our answer to question 2:

$$p(B) - p(A) \geq WTP(B) - WTP(A)$$

If the customer has a lower WTP for company A's product than for company B's product, company A must offer a discount at least as large as its WTP disadvantage: WTP(B) − WTP(A). So, if a customer views company A's product as $3.00 worse than company B's, then company A must have a price at least $3.00 lower than company B's price to win the customer.

In answering these last two questions, note that you can think of WTP advantages and disadvantages in terms of price premiums and discounts. Since some people find this a more intuitive way to think about preference advantages and disadvantages, let's look at it in those terms:

If a company has a WTP advantage, the size of the advantage is equal to the largest price premium it can receive and still sell to the customer.

If a company has a WTP disadvantage, the size of the disadvantage is equal to the smallest price discount it can offer and still sell to the customer.

Two Implicit Assumptions

To summarize, we quantify a given buyer's preference for various products by either calculating or estimating his willingness to pay for the different products. Because companies can change the prices of their products as they compete with one another, the WTP calculation has to be based on alternatives in which prices won't change as the companies compete. We describe such alternatives as *outside* alternatives, short for *alternatives outside the game*. Although we did not emphasize it in our examples above, the WTP calculation is based on the *best* outside alternative. In most contexts we naturally choose the outside alternative that is best, but we make this assumption explicit here.

The other implicit assumption worth noting concerns the applicability of the theory. Whenever we assess a buyer's willingness to pay for a product, we are assuming that there is some dollar amount at which the buyer is indifferent between acquiring the product for that amount and not acquiring the product. This is equivalent to saying that the buyer has a monetary trade-off for the product—that is, the buyer can think in terms of how much money he would trade for the product. But some products are not easily thought of in terms of trade-offs. Prime examples would be necessities such as essential food (e.g., bread and water, not caviar) or medical care (antibiotics, not elective plastic surgery). Some economists believe that there should be a trade-off for everything, but I don't endorse that position. Instead, I recommend that you apply the theory in this book to what constitutes the bulk of business: products for which people do have some choice about whether they need to buy them and, as a consequence, for which there is a price at which they will not buy them.

Economic Cost

In the same way that a buyer has a willingness to pay, a seller has an economic cost. Like willingness to pay, there are contexts in which a seller's economic cost can be subjective and contexts in which it is not. When we use the word "seller," it's important to remember that there are many different kinds of sellers, including companies selling to customers and suppliers selling to companies. An employee is also a seller because she provides a service in return for payment. When employees say that they would do the same job at another company for less pay, they are implicitly saying that they have different economic costs for working at their current company and the other company. And the reason for the difference could be very subjective. I'll provide an example of this later, but just as we did with willingness to pay, we'll start with a minimally subjective example.

Going back to the examples of chapter 2, both ProScan and TechScan had costs of $25 million. As with WTP, economic costs are determined formally by referring to options *outside the game*. Sometimes, though, this formality might not be necessary. We'll start with such an example. In the cost of $25 million, let's say that $15 million represents labor costs and $10 million represents materials costs. Let's also suppose that the seller—say ProScan—has not yet committed to incurring these costs. Then ProScan has the following decision to make:

Status quo alternative: Don't make scanner (and spend nothing)

or

Sell scanner at price p: Receive p and make scanner (pay $15M for labor and $10M for materials)

The seller's economic cost is defined as the price, p, at which it is indifferent between these two choices. By comparing the two choices, we see that ProScan is indifferent between selling the scanner for a price of $25 million and not selling it at all. Its economic cost (and walkaway price) is $25 million.

Economic Cost Is Not Necessarily Production Cost

In this first example, ProScan's economic cost is just its cost of production, and we don't really need to lay out the decision as we did above. But let's now consider two examples that show how economic cost can be counterintuitive. First, suppose that ProScan has already built the scanner and paid the labor and material costs. Suppose, further, that MedCare is the only buyer interested in the scanner. If MedCare doesn't buy the scanner, ProScan will be able to sell the scanner for only the scrap value of the materials in it, say $5M. What is ProScan's economic cost for supplying the scanner? Let's look at ProScan's choices:

Status quo alternative: Scrap scanner and receive $5M

or

Sell scanner at price p: Sell scanner and receive p

Comparing the two choices, we see that the seller is indifferent between selling the scanner for a price of $5 million and not selling it. Therefore, ProScan's economic cost (and walkaway price) is only $5 million. For many students, this is bothersome—they want to account for the $25 million in production costs somehow. But because these costs have already been spent and cannot be retrieved, they are irrelevant to any decision going forward. (Economists would say that the $25 million are "sunk" costs—just like a ship that has sunk and cannot be recovered.)

Let me emphasize why it is important to realize that the seller's economic cost in this situation is $5 million and not, say, $25 million. In the alternative to a deal with MedCare, ProScan will receive $5 million, so any price above $5 million is profit for ProScan. For concreteness, suppose that ProScan (mistakenly) believed its economic cost was $25 million and thus turned down a deal to sell the scanner for, say, $20 million. But selling the scanner for $20 million is a much better outcome than scrapping the scanner for $5 million. So ProScan would have made a bad decision.

The next example is also subtle. Suppose now that ProScan has discovered that its scanner meets the criteria for a scanner that the nationalized health service of a foreign country needs. And this foreign health service has extended a standing offer to buy qualified scanners for $35 million. In this situation, what is ProScan's economic cost for selling a scanner to MedCare?

As before, we look at ProScan's choices:

Status quo alternative: Receive $35M and make scanner (pay $15M for labor and $10M for materials)

or

Sell scanner at price p: Receive p and make scanner (pay $15M for labor and $10M for materials)

Comparing the two choices, we see that ProScan is indifferent between selling the scanner to MedCare at a price of $35 million and the alternative. The seller's economic cost (and walkaway price) is therefore $35 million. For some students, this is still bothersome—as before, the economic cost is not the production cost. But it is clear that ProScan would be foolish to sell the scanner to MedCare for less than $35 million, so developing the intuition for the seller's economic cost is a little easier in this second example.

Economic Cost: The Benchmark May Be Subjective

We now leave the scanner examples and consider a case in which the seller's economic cost can include a significant subjective component. Let's suppose that the seller is an employee, and she is currently working at a company where she is well respected and has friendly coworkers, but she has a long commute to work. Additionally, her salary is

$70,000 a year, and it is fixed at that level due to company policy. Now suppose that a company closer to home approaches her with a job offer. At this new company, she doesn't know how well respected she will be, nor does she know what her coworkers will be like. The question, then, is: What is her economic cost for working at the new company? In other words, what is the smallest salary she would accept to work at the new company? Let's consider her decision:

Status quo alternative: Receive $70,000 per year, be well respected, have good coworkers, have a long commute

or

Work for new company: Receive p per year, be unsure of level of respect, be unsure about coworkers, have a short commute

This decision lays out the issues, and it also shows that more work needs to be done before we can calculate the employee's economic cost for working at the new company. We need to put a dollar amount, in terms of annual salary, on the benefit of friendly coworkers, the benefit of respectful treatment, and the benefit of no commute. Notice that all of these are subjective—they will be based on how the employee values them. Let's suppose that, after much reflection, the employee comes up with the following numbers:

Benefit of knowing that coworkers are friendly: $10,000 per year

Benefit of knowing that treatment is respectful: $10,000 per year

Benefit of no commute: $15,000 per year

The employee might also put a dollar amount, probably negative, on the uncertainty around how well she would be respected at the new company and what her coworkers would be like. Let's say that she views the uncertainty around both these issues at a total negative effect of $5,000 per year. We can now evaluate the employee's decision.

Status quo alternative: Receive $70,000 per year + $10,000/year (friendly coworkers) +$10,000/year (well respected) = $90,000 per year

or

Work for new company: Receive p per year − $5,000/year (uncertainty) + $15,000/year (no commute) = p per year + $10,000 per year

Given these valuations, the employee's economic cost for working at the new company is $80,000 per year. In other words, at any salary above $80,000, she should change jobs and capture p − $80,000 per year in value.

In general, assessing a seller's economic cost tends to be easier than assessing a consumer's willingness to pay. Companies don't like to share cost information, but competitors and consultants are often able to make reasonable estimates of a firm's costs. In situations in which economic costs are difficult to assess, we would like to draw inferences from observed behavior, just as we did above with buyers' willingness to pay. We can do this, but there is one caveat: we must observe a seller who is choosing to sell to one buyer instead of another. In business, this does not happen often because sellers usually want to sell to as many buyers as possible. (If you look back to our willingness-to-pay discussion, you'll note that we had the buyer choosing one product over another. We implicitly ruled out the buyer buying both products.) One context in which a seller might have to choose to sell to one buyer as opposed to another is the one we just looked at: employment. We'll use this context to infer bounds on cost advantages.

Inferring Bounds on Economic Cost: Revealed Preference

These are the two results that parallel the revealed preference results for buyer WTP.

1. If an employee is accepting a lower salary to work for your company versus another company, *the amount of "dislike" for the other company is at least as big as the salary difference.*

2. If an employee is accepting a higher salary to work for your company versus another company, *the "dislike" for your company is no greater than the salary difference.*

The justification for these statements is similar to the justification for the WTP results, so we will do the mathematics only for the first result. Suppose that the employee chooses to work for company A and receives a salary of $p(A)$. Let cost(A) denote her economic cost of working for company A. If she accepts a lower salary than if she worked at company B, this means that $p(A) < p(B)$. Because she prefers more profit to less, it must be the case that she captures more value working at company A than at company B. Thus it must be the case that

$$p(A) - \text{cost}(A) \geq p(B) - \text{cost}(B)$$

Rearranging terms, this is the same as

$$\text{cost}(B) - \text{cost}(A) \geq p(B) - p(A)$$

The salary "discount" she is accepting is a conservative estimate of how much more she would dislike (in terms of salary dollars) working for company B than working for company A. Further, it may be that she would accept an even lower salary from company A before switching to company B, but we don't know this. For an example, let's revisit her decision:

Status quo alternative: Receive $70,000 per year, be well respected, have good coworkers, have a long commute

or

Work for new company: Receive p per year, be unsure of level of respect, be unsure about coworkers, have a short commute

If the employee were not interested in working for the new company at a salary of $100,000, we would know that her economic cost for working at the current company was at least $30,000 lower than for working at the new company. This would imply that the employee views the benefit of being respected and having good coworkers, offset by the hassle of a long commute, to be worth at least $30,000 a year to her.

In the paragraphs above, you may have noticed that I sometimes described economic cost differences as *preference* differences. Rather than saying that the employee had a higher economic cost for working for company B than for company A, I said that the employee *disliked* company B more than company A. You can always interpret economic cost in this way. If you have a lower economic cost for selling your product to firm A than to firm B, you could say that you *prefer* to sell to firm A over firm B. As a practical matter, relating economic costs to preferences seems more natural when a person is involved in the product—say, as an employee or provider of a service—than when the product is a good.

By manipulating the equation $p(A) - cost(A) \geq p(B) - cost(B)$, you can obtain the second result:

$$p(A) - p(B) \geq cost(A) - cost(B)$$

If an employee is accepting a higher salary to work for your company versus another company, *the "dislike" for your company is no greater than the salary difference*. Of course, the employee may even prefer your company. The salary difference provides only a limit on any possible dislike for your company.

Bounds on Salary Premiums and Discounts

Similar to the case of buyer WTP, a seller's economic cost for working for different companies puts bounds on salary premiums and discounts. Because the analysis is symmetric to the analysis of the bounds implied by willingness to pay, I will provide only the two results. (If you want to derive the results yourself, you need only rearrange and interpret the equation $p(A) - cost(A) \geq p(B) - cost(B)$, as we just did above.)

3. If an employee prefers your company over another, you can pay her a lower salary as long as *the difference is smaller than the difference in her economic costs* (between your company and the other company).

4. If an employee prefers another company over yours, you have to pay her a higher salary, where *the difference is at least as big as the difference in her economic costs* (between your company and the other company).

With a better understanding of WTP and economic cost, we explore their role in "winning" a customer in the next chapter.

Appendix: Using Decision Trees in WTP and Economic-Cost Calculations

A decision tree can always be used to illustrate and calculate a buyer's WTP. Here I demonstrate by redoing the first WTP calculation of this chapter. In simple cases, using a decision tree will usually be more complicated than necessary. But for difficult cases, it can help to clarify your thinking.

Consider figure 3.1. The square box in the diagram is the symbol for a decision. Each branch out of the box represents a possible choice. There are two choices: (1) MedCare buys the scanner from ProScan at price WTP and (2) MedCare takes the best course of action "outside of the game," which, in this case, is to maintain the status quo and rent four scanners.

Now, we don't necessarily expect that MedCare will pay its WTP for ProScan's scanner. This decision tree is just a thought experiment to determine MedCare's WTP for ProScan's scanner. To calculate MedCare's WTP in this example, we find the amount at

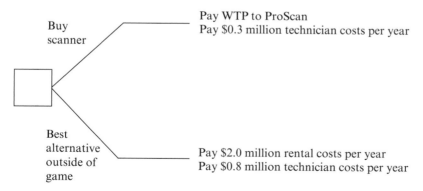

Figure 3.1
Buyer WTP decision tree

which MedCare is indifferent between buying the scanner and using its best outside alternative. Mathematically, this means that we have to find the value of WTP at which the two choices give the same outcome.

To make the point clear, let's re-label the decision tree as in figure 3.2. To find the value for WTP at which these two choices give the same outcome, we make the consequences of these two decisions equal. Thus, we want

– WTP – \$0.3M/year = – \$2.8M/year

Rearranging the terms, this equation simplifies to

WTP = \$2.5M/year

which is what we came up with before. And, as stated earlier, the final step would be to get your finance department to determine how big a one-time payment would be equivalent to a stream of payments of \$2.5 million every year.

For an example of an economic cost calculation, let's revisit the employee's decision:

Status quo alternative: Receive \$70,000 per year + \$10,000/year (friendly coworkers) +\$10,000/year (well respected) = \$90,000 per year

or

Work for new company: Receive cost(new company) per year – \$5,000/year (uncertainty) + \$15,000/year (no commute) = cost(new company) per year + \$10,000 per year

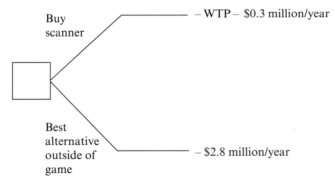

Figure 3.2
Buyer WTP decision tree simplified

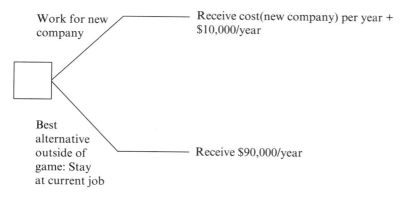

Figure 3.3
Employee economic cost decision tree

Putting this into a decision tree, we get a picture like figure 3.3. To find the employee's economic cost for working for the new company, we make the consequences of these two decisions equal, just as we did in the WTP calculation. Thus, we want

Cost(new company) per year + $10,000/year = $90,000/year

Rearranging the terms, this equation simplifies to

Cost(new company) per year = $80,000/year

which is what we came up with before.

II Being Better—Winning the Customer

4 Competing for the Customer: The Value-Gap Advantage

In chapter 2, we previewed how to successfully compete for a customer. In *Game 2.4*, ProScan had lower costs, and in *Game 2.5*, it had a better product. In this chapter, we will see that lower costs and better products are just special cases of a more general principle: the *value-gap advantage* (*VGA*). I introduced value gaps in chapter 2, and we now explore their central role when companies have to compete for customers—in other words, *when there is excess supply*. Additionally, we'll continue to assume that competition is unrestricted, and, thus, that companies will compete as aggressively as possible.

Value Created with the Customer

To understand value-gap advantages intuitively, consider this simple question: Can you win the customer profitably? The answer is "yes" if you have a value-gap advantage. To see how this works, we revisit *Game 2.4*, depicted in figure 4.1. In that game, ProScan is competing with TechScan for just one customer, MedCare.

As described in chapter 2, a company's value gap with a buyer is simply the buyer's WTP for its product minus the company's economic cost. In *Game 2.4*, ProScan has a value gap of $25 million: $50 million minus $25 million. Note what this value gap of $25 million actually means: if ProScan sells to MedCare, then there will be value creation of $25 million. In other words, this value gap describes the value that ProScan and Medcare can create together. TechScan has a value gap of $30 million: $50 million minus $20M. This is the value that ProScan and MedCare can create together. TechScan's value gap is larger than ProScan's by $5 million, so we say that TechScan has a $5 million *value-gap advantage* over ProScan. In other words, there is $5 million *more* value creation if MedCare transacts with TechScan than if it transacts with ProScan. In figure 4.1, you can see this visually—TechScan's value gap is longer than ProScan's. And

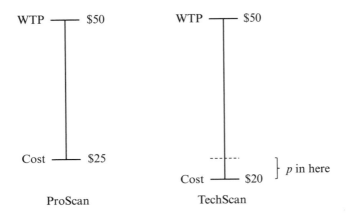

TVC = WTP – cost = $30
MedCare ConV = $30
ProScan ConV = 0
TechScan ConV = $5. This implies p – cost can be up to $5, with p up to $25.

Figure 4.1
Game 2.4 (again)

if the value gaps in the figure were drawn to scale, the extra length would correspond to $5 million.

Because a transaction between TechScan and MedCare creates $5 million more value, we certainly would expect TechScan to make the sale. Let's see why this should be the case. First, a firm's value gap can be thought of as the most value the firm can profitably deliver to the customer. To see this, consider ProScan in figure 4.1. The lowest price at which it does not lose money is its cost, $25 million. If it sells its scanner at this price, then the buyer, MedCare, captures value equal to

WTP – p = $50M – $25M = $25M

Note that this $25 million is equal to ProScan's value gap. Now, to win MedCare as a customer, can TechScan give MedCare *more* than $25 million of value capture and still be profitable? Yes, at any price less than $25 million, MedCare captures more value. And at any price more than $20 million, TechScan makes a profit. Once again, we've reached the same conclusion as in chapter 2: MedCare will buy from TechScan at some price between $20 and $25 million. But we can get to this conclusion directly by thinking in terms of value gaps. First, note that TechScan will make the sale because it has the larger value gap. Second, TechScan's potential profit is the size of its value-gap advantage—$5 million.

In *Game 2.4*, TechScan's value-gap advantage was equal to its cost advantage. In *Game 2.5*, ProScan had the value-gap advantage, and it was equal to its WTP advantage. Figure 4.2 depicts *Game 2.5* again.

The reasoning is conceptually the same as before, but the implication of a difference in willingness to pay is not quite as intuitive as that of a difference in costs. In this game, ProScan has the larger value gap, so it will make the sale. TechScan's value gap is $25 million, so it can deliver $25 million of value capture to MedCare by selling at a price of $25 million. To win the customer, ProScan has to deliver more than $25 million of value to the buyer, which it can, in fact, do. The only wrinkle is that in doing so, it will be pricing *higher* than TechScan's lowest possible price of $25 million. This is not surprising when we remember that the buyer views ProScan's product as $5 million better in this example. But it is important to remember that fact. Figure 4.3 is designed to remind you to think in terms of buyers' value capture rather than prices.

As we noted in chapter 2, these two examples might suggest that value-gap advantages are due either to cost advantages or to WTP advantages. In fact, in the 1980s, some strategists argued that a business's strategy should be either low cost—that is, be a lower cost provider of products/services—or differentiated—that is, have products for

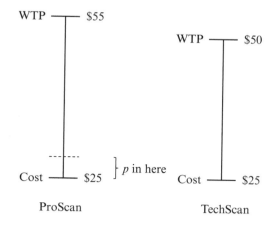

TVC = WTP – cost = $30
MedCare ConV = $30
ProScan ConV = $5. This implies *p* – cost can be up to $5, with *p* up to $30.
TechScan ConV = 0

Figure 4.2
Game 2.5 (again)

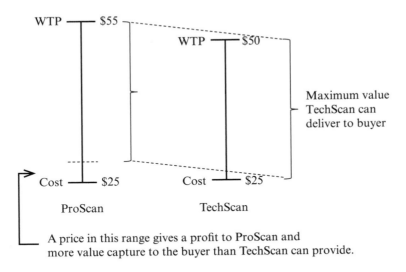

Figure 4.3
Winning the customer

which buyers would have a higher WTP. For some commodity-like products—such as oil, steel, and commodity chemicals—this generic approach to strategy might not lead you astray. But for most businesses, this generic approach doesn't work. Our next game will show why, but it is not hard to think of real-world examples. For instance, there are profitable hotel chains that are neither the lowest cost nor the most luxurious. And many profitable retail clothing businesses have no desire to be either the lowest cost or the most differentiated. One might even argue that the majority of business strategies depend *neither* on being the lowest cost producer nor on being the producer of the most highly differentiated product. Nonetheless, the notions of low cost and differentiation seem like natural business notions, so we need to understand how they relate to profitability. We'll explore this next.

Low Cost, Differentiation, and Profitability

In *Game 4.1*, we will have three companies, unimaginatively called Firm 1, Firm 2, and Firm 3. The three firms make a similar product, but of varying quality—that is, low, medium, and high—and each of the firms is able to produce 15 units of its product. Firm 1 can produce at a cost of $2 per unit, Firm 2 at a cost of $3 per unit, and Firm 3 at a cost of $6 per unit. There are ten buyers in the game, each of which is interested in

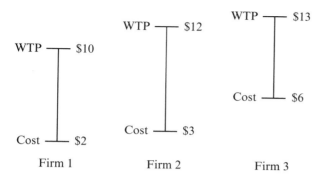

Figure 4.4
Game 4.1

buying only one unit of product from one of the three firms. Each buyer has a WTP of $10 for Firm 1's product, $12 for Firm 2's product, and $13 for Firm 3's product. Figure 4.4 depicts the value gap for each firm.

In contrast to *Games 2.4* and *2.5*, there are now multiple customers, and the companies definitely have to compete for them. Each firm has more than enough capacity (15 units) to serve all the customers, so each firm will try to be the one that serves them all. So, which firm or firms can make a profit in this example? Note that Firm 1 would typically be described as the company with a "low cost" strategy. It has a cost advantage over both its competitors—a $1 advantage over Firm 2 and a $4 advantage over Firm 3. Customers, however, are willing to pay no more than $10 for its product. This gives it a value gap—once again, the difference between its cost and its customers' WTP—of $8. Firm 3, in contrast, follows a differentiated-product strategy, and thus has a WTP advantage over both of its competitors—$1 over Firm 2 and $3 over Firm 3. With a cost of $6, however, it also has a cost disadvantage of $3 with Firm 2 and of $4 with Firm 1. Consequently, at $7, its value gap is even smaller than that of Firm 1. Firm 2's strategy cannot be easily described—it is neither the lowest cost producer nor the company with the best product, where, by "best," I mean the product with the highest buyer WTP. But it is the only company that can make a profit in this example.

If we think in terms of value creation, it is almost obvious why Firm 2 will win all the customers. Its value creation with any given customer is $9 ($12 – $3). This is more value creation than either of the two firms can create with a customer: $8 ($10 – $2) for Firm 1 and $7 ($13 – $6) for Firm 3. So Firm 2 can offer its customers more buyer profit than its competitors can.

For a concrete example of how Firm 2 can win all the customers, suppose that it offered to sell its product for $3.75, giving itself a profit of $.75 per unit. At this price, each customer would capture \$8.25 (= \$12 – \$3.75) of value—more value than the other two firms can provide. Of course, the customers will try to get Firm 2 to sell closer to a price of \$3.00, and Firm 2 will try to get the customers to pay closer to \$4.00. No matter what happens in this bargaining, though, only Firm 2 is in a position to be profitable.

Although Firm 2 was neither the low cost nor the differentiated firm, we can relate these notions to a value-gap advantage—a useful exercise because many people like to think in terms of cost advantages and differentiation. There are two points to keep in mind as you do this. First, think in terms of either a *net* cost advantage or a *net* WTP advantage (or possibly both). Second, and just as important, the type of advantage typically will change firm by firm or competitor by competitor.

In *Game 4.1*, Firm 2 has a value-gap advantage of \$1 over Firm 1. To describe this advantage in terms of cost and WTP advantages (and disadvantages), note that Firm 2 has a cost *disadvantage* and a WTP *advantage* with respect to Firm 1. Because the WTP advantage is larger than the cost disadvantage, we can say that Firm 2 has a *net WTP advantage* with respect to Firm 1 (see figure 4.5). The story is reversed with Firm 3: Firm 2 has a cost *advantage* and a WTP *disadvantage* with respect to Firm 3. Because the WTP disadvantage is smaller than the cost advantage, we can say that Firm 2 has a *net cost advantage* with respect to Firm 3.

Thus, it is meaningless to talk about whether Firm 2 has a low cost or differentiated strategy. Instead, we can say that Firm 2 has a value-gap advantage over its competitors. Alternatively, you could also say that Firm 2 has a net WTP (or differentiation) advantage over Firm 1 *and* a net cost advantage over Firm 3.

At this point, all I have shown is that Firm 2 is the only firm that will have any customers—and thus is the only one with the potential to be profitable. But I haven't said *how* profitable. In part III, you'll see that this sometimes can be a difficult question, but *Game 4.1* has two characteristics that allow me to provide a simple answer. First, since each firm has extra capacity, a buyer always has a credible alternative. Second, each firm has the same cost for each unit it produces, so the cost of, say, the fifth unit it might sell is the same as the cost of the first unit. In economics terms, each firm has *constant marginal costs*. With these two conditions, a firm's maximum possible profit is simply the sum of its value-gap advantages, and its minimum profit is zero. In other words, competition does not guarantee a firm any profit, and the amount that a firm can bargain for equals the sum of its value-gap advantages.

In our example, we saw that that Firm 2 had a value-gap advantage of \$1 over Firm 1 and \$2 over Firm 3. When computing profits due to a value-gap advantage, we compute the advantage over the "next-best" firm. Looking back at figure 4.4 or 4.5,

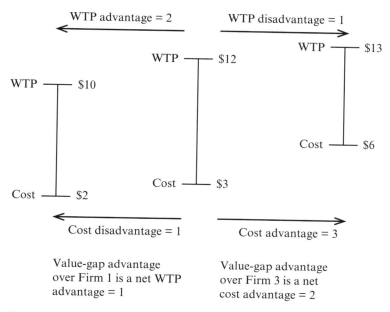

Figure 4.5

Firm 2's value-gap advantages

note that if a customer did not buy from Firm 2, it would create more value with Firm 1 than with Firm 3. So Firm 1 provides the competition for Firm 2. Let's do the calculations.

Firm 2 VGA per customer = ($12 − $3) − ($10 − $2) = $1

Sum of Firm 2 VGA = 10 × Firm 2 VGA per customer = $10

So, on the one hand, Firm 2 could make up to $10. Looking again at figure 4.4 or 4.5, a $10 profit would mean that each customer pays Firm 2 $4. (Remember, if Firm 2 tries to get more than $4 from a customer, the customer will threaten to transact with Firm 1.) On the other hand, Firm 2 could have a profit close to zero. This would occur if Firm 2 were a poor bargainer, and every customer negotiated a price close to $3.

To summarize, if you can create more value with a customer than your competitors can, you will win the customer. Thus, the firm with the largest value gap will win the customer because it can offer the customer the greatest buyer profit *and still remain profitable*.

With unrestricted competition and excess demand, it would appear that we are done. To be profitable, a firm must have a value-gap advantage, but there is one more key point to address: if Firm 2 is the only company that can be profitable in *Game 4.1*, you might then ask why Firms 1 and 3 even exist, or perhaps whether there are any circumstances under which they might realize a profit. To answer those questions, I need to bring buyer segments into our story, which I do next.

5 Customer Tastes and Profitability

In *Game 4.1*, we saw that to win a customer in a competitive environment, more value must be created when the customer transacts with you than with any other competitor. You don't have to have the lowest costs or convince buyers that you offer the best product or service. Rather, you have to provide the most value to the customer while remaining profitable—you need to have the largest value gap. From the example of *Game 4.1*, you might think that there is room for only one "best" company—the one with the largest value gap. But we know from experience that this cannot be the case. After all, many companies find a way to be profitable in the same business. This suggests that I have left something out, and indeed I have. Quite simply, I haven't accounted for the fact that people differ in their tastes.

In all the examples so far, the buyers have had the same tastes. For our purposes, a buyer's tastes are represented by his willingness to pay. If two buyers have the same tastes, then they will have the same WTP for particular products. For instance, in *Game 4.1*, every buyer had the same WTP for Firm 1's product ($10), for Firm 2's product ($12), and for Firm 3's product ($13). Thus, all the buyers had the same tastes in that game. When a group of buyers share the same tastes, we say that they are in the same *buyer segment*. However, in most markets, buyers will differ significantly in their tastes, so there will be multiple buyer segments. In this chapter, you'll see that this is fortunate for business. With multiple buyer segments, more than one company can be profitable, even if there is an excess of supply among all the companies.

I'll demonstrate the role of buyer segments with a game that builds upon *Game 4.1*. Recall that in *Game 4.1*, Firm 2 had the largest value gap and was the only profitable company. *Game 5.1* will feature the same three firms, each making the same product, each with the same costs, and each with a capacity of 15 units of product. *Game 5.1* differs from *Game 4.1* in only one respect: it has 30 buyers instead of 10. These buyers consist of three equal-sized segments (one of which will be identical to the original buyer group in *Game 4.1*). To emphasize that buyer segments are a way to account for differences in taste, let's give each firm a concrete product: chairs. Firm 3 makes a premium chair, Firm 2 a standard chair, and Firm 1 a bean bag chair. There will be a *Luxury* segment, a *Standard* segment, and a *"Retro"* segment. The buyers in the Standard segment are identical to the ten buyers in *Game 4.1*. The Luxury segment is the same as the Standard segment but with one difference: a Luxury buyer is willing to pay more for a premium chair: $16 rather than the $13 a Standard buyer would pay. A Retro buyer is willing to pay $16 for a premium chair as well but is willing to pay $1 less for a Standard chair. But the biggest difference between a Retro buyer and those in the other two segments is that a Retro buyer finds a bean bag chair desirable, while Luxury and Standard buyers view it as inferior.

With different buyer segments, we need a more complicated picture to depict the situation. Although there are only three firms, we have to account for the fact that each buyer segment has a different WTP for each of the firms, and thus a different perspective on the products or services they offer. Figure 5.1 shows one way to do this. Each box corresponds to a buyer segment and contains a set of value sticks for the buyer segment. Now remember that while there are only three firms, for each firm there has to be a value stick for each of the three segments. In other words, figure 5.1 depicts each segment's perspective on the three firms. (In teaching, we call pictures like figure 5.1 *Rashomon* diagrams, after the Japanese film classic of that name. In that movie all the witnesses to a murder recount different perspectives on the *same* crime. In much the same way, each buyer segment *sees* the value of the three firms' products differently.)

We can use figure 5.1 to see which companies will be profitable. From our analysis of *Game 4.1*, we already know that Firm 2 will be profitable in the Standard segment, as it has the largest value gap in that segment. What about the Retro segment? Here, Firm 1 has a value gap ($12 = $14 − $2) larger than Firm 2's ($8 = $11 − $3) and Firm 3's ($10 = $16 − $6). Thus, Firm 1 will win the Retro segment. Moreover, as we saw in chapter 4, its profitability will be based on its value-gap advantage over the company with the next-largest value gap. In the Retro segment, this is Firm 3, with a value gap of $10, implying that Firm 1 has a value-gap advantage of $2.00. If Firm 1 captures its value-gap advantage, it will make $2.00 per unit, or $20 in total. Additionally, note that a profit of $2.00 per unit translates into a price of $4.00 per unit. At this price, each buyer in the Retro segment is guaranteed to capture $10. If a Retro buyer can negotiate a lower price with Firm 1, it could get as much as $12 in buyer profit. Figure 5.2 provides a visual representation of the value-gap advantages. The length of the next-longest

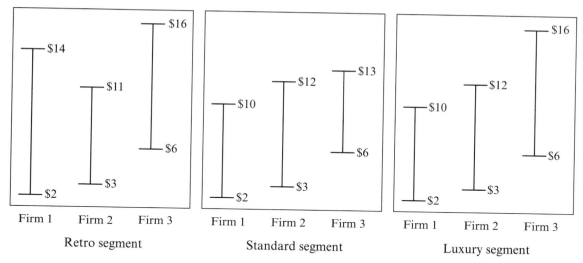

Figure 5.1

How the buyer segments view the three firms

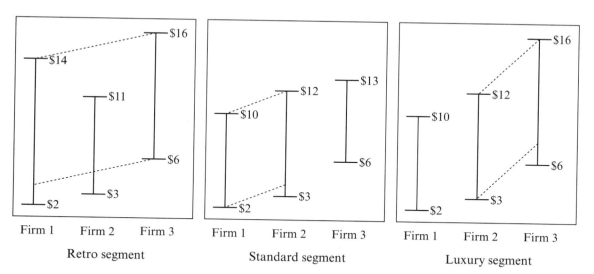

Figure 5.2

Value-gap advantages by segment

value gap is superimposed on the longest value gap. The remaining difference is the firm's potential profit.

We haven't discussed the Luxury segment yet, so let's use figure 5.2. As the figure shows, in the Luxury segment, Firm 3 has the largest value gap, $10 (= $16 − $6). The next-largest is Firm 2's value gap of $9 (= $12 − $3), implying that Firm 3 has a value-gap advantage of $1.00 in the Luxury segment. If Firm 3 captures its value-gap advantage, it will make $1.00 per unit, or $10.00 total. A profit of $1 per unit translates into a price of $7 per unit. At this price, each Luxury buyer is guaranteed to capture $9. And if a Luxury buyer can negotiate a lower price with Firm 3, it can get as much as $10 in buyer profit.

Note that all the buyers view the premium chair as the best chair—they all have the highest willingness to pay for the premium chair. But as the analysis above shows, this is not the most important fact to a buyer. The value that a firm can deliver to the buyer—the firm's value gap with the buyer—is what's important.

Interdependency of Competition

Figure 5.2 provides a good opportunity to make an interesting observation about the nature of competition. In this example, think of each company as targeting a different buyer segment. Firm 1 targets Retro buyers with a low cost product (the bean bag chair). Firm 2 targets buyers who are willing to pay for a standard product, and perhaps a bit more for a premium product. Consequently, it has a more expensive manufacturing process than Firm 1 has. Firm 3 targets buyers who will pay a lot for a premium product. Its manufacturing process is much more expensive, and it produces a product that the Luxury segment strongly prefers. Each company targets a different segment of buyers, and this allows each to make a profit. But here is the interesting observation: Though each company targets a different segment, each may be a source of competition in another segment.

To see this in our example, consider the Retro segment. Firm 1 will win the buyers in this segment, but why can it make, at most, only $2 per unit? The answer: if it tries to make more than that, Firm 3 could step in and take the customer. Remember, Firm 3 has extra capacity: it can sell up to 15 units, but it will sell only 10 of these to its target segment, the Luxury buyers. So if Firm 1 gets too greedy with one of its target customers, Firm 3 will happily serve that customer. Thus, Firm 3 provides competitive pressure in the Retro segment, even though it has no intention of selling to this segment. Mathematically, we accounted for this when we said that a value-gap advantage was based on the advantage over the company with the next-largest value gap. Looking at figure

5.2, we can see that Firm 3 provides the competitive pressure in the Retro segment; Firm 1 provides the competitive pressure in the Standard segment; and Firm 2 provides the competitive pressure in the Luxury segment.

As an aside, this is another benefit of Rashomon-style figures—namely figures 5.2 and 5.3. In addition to emphasizing the fact that different buyer segments may value a company's products differently, they remind us about the interactive nature of competition. In particular, competition for your company's products could easily come from a competitor whose strategy does not target your customers.

Potential Profits

We'll finish by computing the maximum possible profit that each firm can make in this example. I've already presented the answer both verbally and visually, so here are the equations.

The sum of Firm 1's value-gap advantages is $20:

Firm 1 VGA per customer = ($14 − $2) − ($16 − $6) = $2.00

Sum of Firm 1 VGA = 10 × Firm 1 VGA per customer = $20

The sum of Firm 2's value-gap advantages is $10:

Firm 2 VGA per customer = ($12 − $3) − ($10 − $2) = $1.00

Sum of Firm 2 VGA = 10 × Firm 2 VGA per customer = $10

The sum of Firm 3's value-gap advantages is also $10:

Firm 3 VGA per customer = ($16 − $6) − ($12 − $3) = $1.00

Sum of Firm 3 VGA = 10 × Firm 3 VGA per customer = $10

Summary of Our Main Result for Part II

If you have to compete for customers, if competition is unrestricted, and if you want to be profitable, then

You must identify customer segments in which you have the largest value gap.

For a more formal statement of this result, we need to be more precise about the phrase 'have to compete for customers.' Throughout part II, I've used this phrase to summarize two assumptions: that every firm has extra capacity and that every firm has constant marginal costs—that is, for each firm, the cost per unit does not depend on how many units the firm produces. With these two assumptions, and if competition is unrestricted, we have the following three facts:

1. No firm is guaranteed a profit due to competition.
2. If a firm has segments in which it has the largest value gap, then it can bargain for a potential profit.
3. To calculate this potential profit, for each buyer (with whom it has the largest value gap), compute the firm's value-gap advantage over whichever firm has the next-largest value gap with the buyer. The sum of these advantages is the firm's potential profit.

Appendix: Contributed Value and Value-Gap Advantages

The examples in chapter 2 relied on the contributed value of each player in our analysis, while those in chapters 4 and 5 relied on value-gap advantages. As long as each firm has plenty of excess capacity, these two approaches produce the same results. But when firms have only a little extra capacity, or even none, it will not be enough to consider the individual players' contributed values. We will also have to consider the contributed values of groups of players. The fact that a group of players cannot capture more than it contributes will sometimes imply that an individual player will not be able to capture its contributed value. In this appendix, I provide some intuition into this phenomenon by considering two variants of a game we've already analyzed—*Game 4.1.*

Example: When a Firm's Contributed Value Equals Value-Gap Advantages

Recall that each of the firms is able to produce 15 units of its product and that there are 10 buyers in the game, each of which is interested in buying only one unit of product

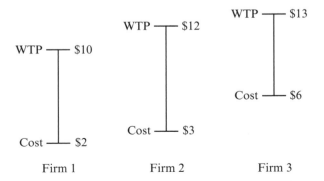

Figure 5.3
Game 4.1

from one of the three firms. Using value-gap advantages, we determined that Firm 2 would be the only firm that could make a profit, and its maximum possible profit was $10:

Firm 2 VGA per customer = ($12 − $3) − ($10 − $8) = $1

Sum of Firm 2 VGA = 10 × Firm 2 VGA per customer = $10

Let's use a contributed-value analysis, as in chapter 2. We have ten buyers, so only ten units will be sold. From our analysis of the value gaps, the largest amount of value will be created if the buyers purchase from Firm 2. Therefore, the total value created in the game is:

TVC = 10 × ($12 − $3) = $90

Because neither Firm 1 nor Firm 3 is involved in the total value created, we know that each will have a contributed value of zero. What, therefore, is Firm 2's contributed value? Put another way, without Firm 2, how could the greatest value be created in the game? From our earlier value-gap analysis, we know that Firm 1 had the next-largest value gap. So, without Firm 2, the greatest possible value creation involves customers doing business with Firm 1.

Firm 2 ConV = TVC − Value created w/o Firm 2
            = $90 − 10 × ($10 − $2) = $90 − $80 = $10

Firm 2's contributed value is $10—the same as the sum of its value-gap advantages. So, in this example, Firm 2 could possibly capture its contributed value.

Example: When a Firm's Contributed Value Overstates Its Value-Gap Advantages

Now let's modify the game slightly. Suppose, as before, that Firm 2 can produce up to 15 units. But now suppose that Firm 1 can produce just *one* unit, and Firm 3 can no longer produce any units. Perhaps surprisingly, this does not affect Firm 2's profits. As long as Firm 1 has just one unit it would not sell otherwise, this one unit will provide competition for Firm 2 in dealing with all ten buyers. Consequently, Firm 2 will be able to capture only $10, just as before.

But look at what happens to the contributed-value calculation. Without Firm 2, only one unit will be sold (by Firm 1):

Firm 2 ConV = TVC − Value created w/o Firm 2
            = $90 − 1 × ($10 − $2) = $90 − $8 = $82

Firm 2's contributed value is $82. This far exceeds the $10 that Firm 2 could capture.

Conceptually, considering the contributed values of individual players is an essential first step. It captures the intuition that to be profitable, you must contribute to the overall value creation. And it sometimes suffices to explain what can happen. For instance, if each firm has constant marginal costs and the capacity to serve all the buyers, then contributed values will explain how competition works. (These conditions are met in the original version of *Game 4.1*.) But the effects of competition often limit one's ability to capture what one contributes. The contributed value of a group of players will limit a player's ability to capture its contributed value. Understanding this fact will give you a deeper understanding of the way that competition can guarantee some profitability, as well as of the emergence of market prices, a phenomenon we will introduce in part III.

III Being in Demand

6   Guaranteed Profitability: The Power of Exclusion

In part II, we discussed how to win customers profitably when you have to compete for them. You have to be better than your competitors, with "better" measured in terms of your value creation with your customer—meaning your value gap. But successfully competing for a customer doesn't guarantee that you will make any money from that person. In fact, in every example except *Game 2.2*, the firm that won the customers still had to bargain for its profits. We know that both competition and bargaining determine profits, and in those examples, while competition did not guarantee any profit to the firm, it did guarantee profit to the buyers. In this part of the book, we'll look at the ways in which competition can guarantee profits to a firm. You'll see how the force of competition can benefit not only a firm with the largest value gap in a segment, but also firms that are "inferior." In other words, we will see how a firm can be profitable even if it cannot identify segments in which it has the largest value gap.

An Excluded Buyer

Consider, once again, *Game 2.5*. Recall that ProScan will successfully compete for the customer—MedCare. But to make a profit, ProScan has to negotiate for a price above $25 million. As mentioned above, profits are usually determined by both competition and bargaining, but in this game, competition does not guarantee ProScan any profit. If ProScan wants to make a significant profit, it must negotiate for a price much higher than $25 million, ideally a price close to $30 million.

But if we consider the buyer—MedCare—in this game, we do see the force of competition. Because the buyer is guaranteed a price no higher than $30 million, it is guaranteed a profit of at least $25 million. The reason for this guaranteed profit is the competition between ProScan and TechScan. Although it is intuitive, we need to ask exactly what the nature of competition is. In this chapter and the next, you'll see that the essential idea behind competition acting in your favor is *exclusion*. In *Game 2.5*,

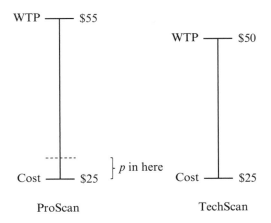

TVC = WTP – cost = $30
MedCare ConV = $30
ProScan ConV = $5. This implies p – cost can be up to $5, wirh p up to $30.
TechScan ConV = 0

Figure 6.1
Game 2.5

TechScan will be excluded from the final deal with MedCare. Because of this fact, MedCare is guaranteed a profit in its transaction with ProScan.

Let's now return to the firm's perspective. In *Game 2.2*, competition guaranteed all of the profits to the firm, so let's review that example. That game had two buyers—MedCare and HealthCo—but only one seller—ProScan. Because ProScan had only one unit, one of the buyers had to be excluded.

Using contributed values, we saw that ProScan would capture all the value, implying a price of $50 million. Because each buyer contributed zero value, the seller captured all of the pie. If you recall, each buyer's zero contributed value was due to an excluded buyer. An excluded buyer is always willing to take the place of an included buyer—namely a buyer transacting with the firm. And if an excluded buyer could create just as much value with the firm as the included buyer, then the included buyer will capture nothing. Thus, the firm will capture all of the value in the deal with the included buyer.

Game 2.2 is a little confusing in that it doesn't matter which buyer transacts with ProScan. (If MedCare transacts with ProScan, then HealthCo is excluded; if HealthCo transacts with ProScan, then MedCare is excluded.) In the next example, we give

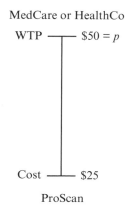

MedCare or HealthCo

WTP —— $50 = p

Cost —— $25

ProScan

TVC = WTP − cost = $25
MedCare ConV = 0. HealthCo ConV = 0. This implies p = WTP = $50.
ProScan ConV = $25
ProScan Profit = p − cost = $25

Figure 6.2
Game 2.2

each buyer a different willingness to pay, so the effect of the excluded buyer should be easier to see.

In *Game 6.1*, we now suppose that ProScan can produce three scanners instead of one. The game will have four buyers, each with a different WTP for a ProScan scanner. Figure 6.3 depicts how each buyer views a ProScan scanner. (Each buyer has a willingness to pay for only one scanner.)

Because ProScan has only three scanners, one buyer will clearly be excluded. Because Buyer 4 would create the smallest value with ProScan, it will be excluded. Unlike *Game 2.2*, though, the excluded buyer cannot create as much value with ProScan as any of the included buyers. Consequently, Buyers 1, 2, and 3 contribute value and have the chance for profitability: ProScan will have to do some bargaining to capture all of its potential profit.

But ProScan is guaranteed *some* profit. Buyer 4, because it is excluded, would always be willing to pay a price of, say, $34.95 million rather than be excluded. Knowing this, ProScan would not accept a price less than $35 million from any of the remaining buyers. Thus, ProScan is guaranteed a price of $35 million, implying a profit of $10 million per unit. Because ProScan will sell three units, it has a guaranteed profit of $30 million in this game.

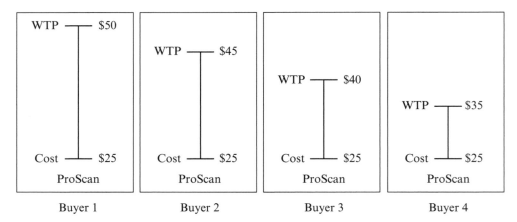

Figure 6.3
Game 6.1

Note that the threat from Buyer 4—the excluded buyer—affects *all* of the buyers transacting with ProScan. This is one of the central features of how competition works, and we sometimes call it the "musical chairs" aspect of competition. In fact, if you played musical chairs as a child, you should have a visceral understanding of unrestricted competition.

In the game of musical chairs, a group of players (usually children) circle around a collection of chairs while some music plays. When the music stops (without warning), every child has to find a chair to sit in. The wrinkle in the game is that there is always one fewer chair than there are children. One of the intriguing aspects of this game is that even with a reasonable number of children—say, about 16—each child will worry that she will be the one to get shut out of a chair, even though for any given child, this is an unlikely occurrence. (There are 15 chairs after all.) For our purposes, the key insight is that *all* the players feel the shortage of just *one* chair.

Impact of an Excluded Buyer on the Contributed Values of Included Buyers

By looking at the impact of an excluded buyer on the included buyers, we can actually see the musical chairs effect. The pie is the value that ProScan creates with Buyers 1, 2, and 3:

TVC = ($50M − $25M) + ($45M − $25M) + ($40M − $25M) = $60M

To compute the contributed values of Buyers 1 through 3, we merely need to note the difference in value creation if the buyer is replaced by Buyer 4:

Buyer 1 ConV = $15M (Buyer 1's WTP is $15M greater than Buyer 4's WTP)

Buyer 2 ConV = $10M (Buyer 2's WTP is $10M greater than Buyer 4's WTP)

Buyer 3 ConV = $5M (Buyer 3's WTP is $5M greater than Buyer 4's WTP)

Buyer 4 ConV = 0 (Buyer 4 is not part of the total value created)

You can begin to see the musical chairs in the equations above. Buyer 1 creates $25 million with ProScan, but it contributes only $15 million. The reason? Buyer 4. Similarly, Buyer 2 creates $20 million with ProScan, but it contributes only $10 million. Buyer 4 is again the reason. While buyers 1 through 3 may not be worried about having "a chair to sit in," each is worried that ProScan might transact with Buyer 4. Even though there is just *one* excluded buyer (Buyer 4), *all* of ProScan's buyers feel the effect of this excluded buyer.

By adding up the contributed values of the buyers, we know that the most the buyers can capture, collectively, is $30 million. Because there is a $60 million pie, ProScan must be guaranteed $30 million, as I argued above.

Remember, $30 million is only ProScan's *guaranteed* profit. It can negotiate for an additional $15 million from Buyer 1, an additional $10 million from Buyer 2, and an additional $5 million from Buyer 3. Thus, ProScan is guaranteed a profit of $30 million and can negotiate for up to $30 million more, giving it a potential profit of $60 million.

Emergence of Price-Setting Power

Let me emphasize two more points in this example. The first is the connection between guaranteed profit and price-setting power. ProScan's guaranteed profit of $30 million is based on a price of $35 million per unit. Because this is the lowest price that ProScan can get (with unrestricted competition), we can say that competition gives ProScan the power to set a price of $35 million. More generally, we can say that

If competition guarantees a profit to a firm, then competition gives it the power to set a price consistent with the guaranteed profit.

With unrestricted competition, we never start out assuming that any player has price-setting power. But as this example shows, price-setting power can emerge. The key point to remember, though, is that with unrestricted competition, price-setting power, if it exists, is a consequence of the force of competition.

For this reason, to understand when a firm is guaranteed a profit, it suffices to understand when competition gives a firm the power to set a price and what the price will be. In the example above, you might have noticed that ProScan's guaranteed price—$35 million—was the same as the excluded buyer's (Buyer 4's) willingness to pay. This brings us to the second point to I want to emphasize:

Conditional on winning customers, a firm can always charge a price equal to the willingness to pay of an excluded buyer.

This is the simplest way to understand the power of exclusion, and in this chapter's appendix, I show that traditional supply and demand reasoning rests on this simple fact.

Exclusion Can Benefit All Competitors

In *Game 6.1*, the seller, ProScan, faced no competition. You might think that the benefit of an excluded buyer would be diminished in the presence of a competitor, but this is not the case. As long as there is an excluded buyer, a firm can set a price equal to at least the willingness to pay of the excluded buyer. In *Game 6.2*, we bring back TechScan to illustrate this point. We now assume that ProScan can produce four scanners, and we additionally assume that TechScan can produce four scanners as well. To make the game more interesting, we have three segments of three buyers each—Pros, Techs, and Neutrals—for a total of nine buyers. Because there are only eight scanners in total, we

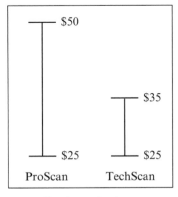 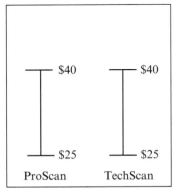 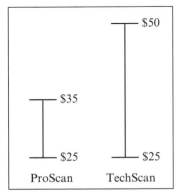

Pro buyer's view   Neutral buyer's view   Tech buyer's view

Figure 6.4
Game 6.2

know that there will be one excluded buyer. Figure 6.3 depicts each segment's view of the two firms.

In this game, the excluded buyer is one of the Neutral buyers. ProScan will transact with all of the Pro buyers and one of the Neutral buyers; TechScan will transact with all of the Tech buyers and one of the Neutral buyers. The remaining Neutral buyer will be excluded, and thus both ProScan and TechScan will have the power to set a price at the Neutral buyer's WTP: $40 million. Consequently, ProScan and TechScan are guaranteed a profit of at least $15 million per scanner for a total of $60 million each.

This last example demonstrates once again the power of the musical chair phenomenon—that is, the power of having just slightly more demand than can be served. Just one extra buyer—one of the Neutral Buyers—provides competitive pressure on all of ProScan's customers *and* all of TechScan's customers.

As both *Games 6.1* and *6.2* show, excluded buyers can guarantee profits to a firm. Because an excluded buyer is a form of excess demand, this should seem intuitive. If buyers have to compete for your products, you would expect that this should lead to a higher price for your products, and, consequently, guaranteed profits.

In the business world, though, this often seems to be an unusual case. Businesses tend to feel that they have to compete for customers, not that customers have to compete for them. Fortunately, there is a sense in which customers might have to compete for your firm's product, even if there appear to be more than enough competing products for all the possible buyers. I show how this works in the next chapter.

Appendix: Monopoly Power and Supply-Demand Reasoning

In this appendix, I show how excluded players can explain both monopoly power and traditional supply and demand reasoning. Let's start with monopoly.

Recall that in *Game 6.1* we had one firm—ProScan, which could supply three scanners—and four buyers, each of whom wanted one scanner. Each buyer had a different willingness to pay for a scanner, so there were four segments of one buyer each. Accordingly, figure 6.3 provided each buyer's value gap. But there is another standard way to depict this sort of game, as figure 6.5 shows.

In the figure the solid line is the buyers' willingnesses to pay plotted together in what is called a *demand curve*. The line with the large dashes represents ProScan's *cost curve*. For instance, ProScan can produce one unit at a cost of $25 million, a second unit at a cost of $25 million, and a third unit at a cost of $25 million. Notice that in the figure, ProScan's cost for the fourth unit is effectively infinite: it is off the chart, both

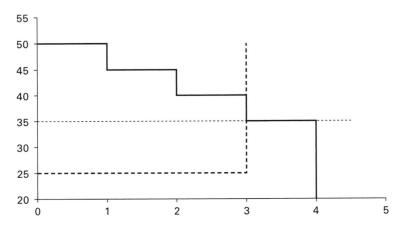

Figure 6.5
Traditional monopoly picture for *Game 6.1*

literally and figuratively. This is because ProScan has a capacity of just three in the example.

The line with small dashes is drawn at the willingness to pay of the excluded buyer. In our analysis of *Game 6.1*, we determined that the pie was $60 million, that ProScan was guaranteed a profit of $30 million, that it could bargain for another $30 million, and that the contributed values of Buyers 1, 2, and 3 were $15M, $10M, and $5M, respectively. All of these values can be seen in figure 6.6. The pie is the area between the demand curve and the cost curve. ProScan's guaranteed profit is the area between the cost curve and the short-dashed line. The extra profit that ProScan can bargain for is the area between the demand curve and the short-dashed line. And a buyer's contributed value is the area directly below its willingness to pay, ending at the short-dashed line.

Monopoly

We can use a picture like the one in figure 6.5 to understand the main issue with a monopoly firm. To make the pictures dramatic, we will use an example with ten buyers instead of four and with buyer willingnesses to pay ranging from $14 million down to $5 million. We'll consider just one simple question: How much capacity would the firm like to have? Let's start by supposing that the seller could supply all ten buyers at a cost per unit of $4 million. Figure 6.7 depicts this first scenario.

There are two things to notice about this scenario. The first is that the pie is as large as it can be—$55 million. The second is that the firm is not guaranteed any profit. It

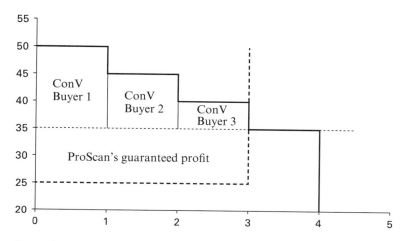

Figure 6.6
Division of value created

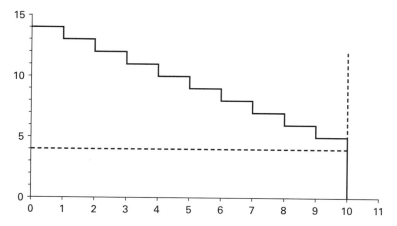

Figure 6.7
Monopolist supplies all buyers

must bargain for its profits, as must the buyers. So the firm could get the whole pie, none of the pie, or some amount in between. The important point to realize in this scenario is that there is no "monopoly power." Although there is one firm and many buyers, the firm will essentially be in ten one-on-one negotiations with the buyers.

Now let's suppose instead that the firm can supply only nine units. In figure 6.8, we have an excluded buyer, so now the firm is guaranteed a profit of $9 million. The pie has shrunk a bit—it is $1 million smaller—and unless the firm is an amazing bargainer, this is probably better for the firm.

In figure 6.9, the firm can supply only five units. The firm's guaranteed profit is now $25 million, but the pie has shrunk to $40 million. Is this better than supplying ten units? It depends upon how good a bargainer the firm believes it is. For instance, let's suppose that the firm believes it can capture 75 percent of the negotiable value in any deal. If it supplies ten units, it would expect a profit of 75 percent of $55 million—or $41.25 million. If it supplies five units, it would expect a profit of $25 million plus 75 percent of $15 million—or $36.75 million. So, based on its optimistic view of its negotiation skills, the firm might sacrifice guaranteed profitability for the chance to negotiate for a bigger piece of a bigger pie.

Figure 6.10 plots the firm's guaranteed and potential profit for each capacity choice. If a firm is pessimistic about its bargaining ability, it will try to maximize its guaranteed profit. In this example, the firm would likely provide five units. The more optimistic the firm is about its bargaining ability, the more units it will provide.

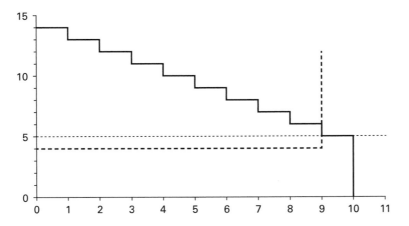

Figure 6.8
One buyer excluded

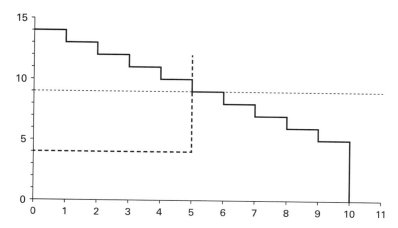

Figure 6.9
Five buyers excluded

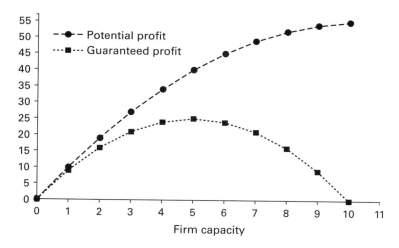

Figure 6.10
Profit implications of different capacity choices

A monopolist, then, has power only if it can credibly undersupply the market. The undersupply creates excluded buyers, and excluded buyers create competition for the firm. As a result of this buyer competition, the firm is guaranteed profits. Alternatively, buyer competition gives the firm the power to credibly set a price equal to the willingness to pay of the just-excluded buyer. In short, monopoly is a story of *one-sided* competition, where the only "side" competing is the buyer side.

Supply and Demand

The standard supply and demand story is just *two-sided* competition. Again, I'll demonstrate with an example. Figure 6.11 depicts a game with five buyers and five sellers. Each buyer is interested in only one unit, and the demand curve in the figure describes the willingnesses to pay. Each seller has only one unit to sell, and each has a different cost. The cost curve in the figure depicts these costs. Because the cost curve includes the costs of more than one firm, we call it a supply curve. Note that in this game, there is an excluded seller—the seller with a cost of $7 million—as well as an excluded buyer—the buyer with a willingness to pay of $6 million.

Before analyzing this game, it is useful to note why we can draw a picture with supply and demand curves rather than with value gaps for each buyer segment. (In this example, there are five segments of one buyer each. In a diagram with value gaps, there would be five sets of five value gaps.) *We can draw a demand curve because a buyer's willingness to pay for a product does not depend on which firm produced it.* And *we can draw a*

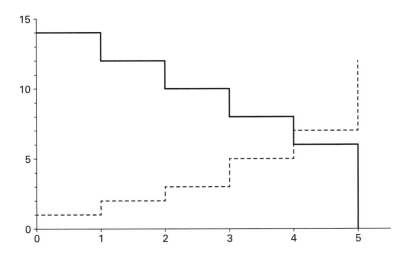

Figure 6.11
Traditional supply and demand game

cost curve because each seller's cost does not depend on whom it sells to. The first of these two conditions is particularly restricting—we typically do care about which firm makes a product that interests us. But when these two conditions hold, we can draw a supply and demand curve instead of value gaps.

Now let's look at the analysis. This game has an excluded buyer, so we know that each seller will be guaranteed a price equal to the willingness to pay of the excluded buyer. This guarantees profit to the sellers, as depicted by the dark regions in figure 6.12. Moreover, each seller might be able to bargain for more, as depicted by the arrows.

But shouldn't the excluded seller be a source of competition that benefits the buyers? The answer is yes. Consider the contributed value of the lowest cost seller; without this seller, the excluded seller would take its place. Because the excluded seller's cost is $6 million greater than that of the lowest cost seller, the contributed value of the lowest cost seller is $6 million. Because the lowest cost seller cannot capture more than its contributed value, we know that the highest price that the lowest cost seller can get is $7 million.

If you do the contributed value calculations for the other three sellers, you'll find that the highest price that any of them could receive is also $7 million. The maximum price for all four sellers is $7 million. Put another way, each buyer is *guaranteed* to pay no more than $7 million. More generally, each buyer has a *guaranteed profit* equal to its willingness to pay minus the cost of the excluded seller; see figure 6.13.

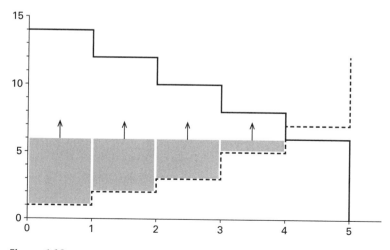

Figure 6.12
Sellers' guaranteed profits

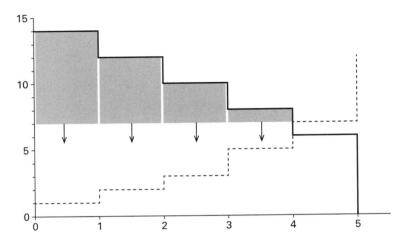

Figure 6.13
Buyers' guaranteed profits

Thus, the benefit of an excluded seller to buyers is symmetric to the benefit of an excluded buyer to sellers. If we put figures 6.12 and 6.13 together, we see that prices must be between $6 million and $7 million, and, as figure 6.14 shows, this range is where the supply and demand curves intersect. Thus, when someone draws supply and demand curves and claims that prices will be at their intersection, contributed values alone can easily justify this claim. Furthermore, the reason for these prices is simply two-sided competition.

As a final note, the analysis above used only the contributed values of individual players to show that the goods would be exchanged at prices between $6 million and $7 million. But if we also consider the contributed values of groups of players, we can actually make a stronger statement: a *single* (uniform) price will emerge. The price will still be in the same range, but the surprising fact is that everyone will pay the same price. To prove this in general is difficult, but I can give you the flavor of how the proof works. Consider a simplified version of figure 6.11 with just three buyers and three sellers.

Suppose that Buyer 1 pays a higher price, say p, than Buyer 2 pays, say, q. Now consider the value that Buyer 2 and Seller 1 capture:

$$(\$8 - q) + (p - \$3) = \$5 + (p - q) > \$5$$

But the value that Buyer 2 and Seller 1 contribute as a pair is

$$[(\$10 - \$3) + (\$8 - \$5)] - (\$10 - \$5) = \$5$$

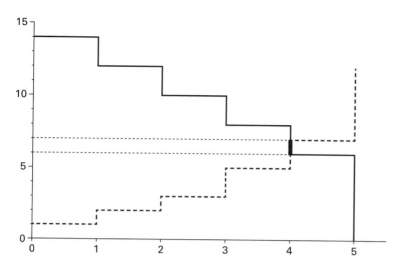

Figure 6.14
Supply and demand intersection

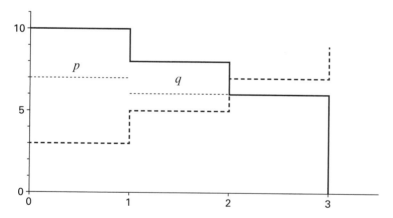

Figure 6.15
Outcome incompatible with unrestricted competition

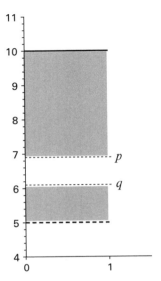

Figure 6.16
A good deal left undone

Thus, Buyer 2 and Seller 1 capture more value than they contribute. Because this cannot happen with unrestricted competition, the price must be the same (with unrestricted competition).

Figure 6.15 also suggests a visual reason why there cannot be different prices in this game. In figure 6.16, I put Buyer 1's value capture with Seller 2's value capture. The gap in the middle represents additional value that Buyer 1 and Seller 2 could capture by doing a deal on their own. With different prices in this game, there would always be a pair of players that could do better on their own—a good deal would be left "undone." So, again, unrestricted competition implies that a uniform price will emerge in this type of situation.

7 Envy Is a Form of Exclusion

In the last chapter, we saw how beneficial an excluded buyer could be. An excess of buyers—in fact, just one excess buyer—guaranteed that buyers would have to compete for firms' products, which, in turn, guaranteed profitability for the firms. But few businesses feel that they are lucky enough to be in such a situation. Typically, there is always some competitor ready to take your place with any of your customers. Rather than there being excluded buyers, it always seems as if some firm has extra capacity. Demand doesn't exceed supply; rather, supply exceeds demand.

In this chapter, you'll see how, even with excess supply, there can be competition for your firm's product. At first, this will probably strike you as a little strange—how can buyers be competing for your product when every buyer is being served? But, in fact, this makes perfect sense. Quite simply, a competitor's buyer might prefer to transact with your firm—that is, someone else's buyer might feel *excluded from your firm*. What, precisely, does "prefer to transact with your firm" mean? Fortunately, you'll see that this is just a matter of understanding a buyer's value creation with a firm, something with which you're already familiar. And it might seem curious that your firm could benefit from a competitor's buyer—the competitor will not be helping us, but its customers certainly could be. Let's call such buyers—who act very much like excluded buyers—*envious* buyers. In short, envy is a form of exclusion. Understanding this fact is the key to understanding how a firm is guaranteed a profit even when there is an excess of supply for all the buyers.

In *Game 7.1*, there are two buyers, a chocolate lover and a chocolate connoisseur. The lover likes both dark chocolate and milk chocolate, while the connoisseur likes only dark chocolate. There are two firms—one makes only dark chocolate, and the other makes only milk chocolate. We assume that the dark-chocolate firm can supply, at most, one of the buyers, but the milk-chocolate firm can supply both buyers. Thus,

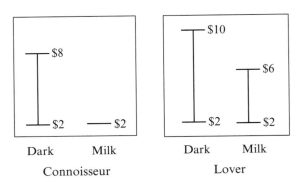

Figure 7.1
Game 7.1

we have extra supply—the two companies together could serve up to three buyers, but there are only two available. Figure 7.1 depicts the value gaps for the two buyers.

The Excluded Chocolate Lover

The chocolate lover clearly prefers dark chocolate to milk chocolate, and she is willing to pay more for dark chocolate than the connoisseur is willing to pay. So you might expect that she will be the one to buy the dark chocolate. But she won't. She will end up buying milk chocolate and will provide a source of competition that benefits the dark-chocolate company. To understand why, it's helpful to first compute the pie. There are two scenarios in which value can be created in this situation: The chocolate lover buys dark chocolate, and the connoisseur buys milk chocolate; or the chocolate lover buys milk chocolate, and the connoisseur buys dark chocolate. Here is the value that would be created in these two scenarios:

Lover & Dark + Connoisseur & Milk = (10 − 2) + 0 = $8

Lover & Milk + Connoisseur & Dark = (6 − 2) + (8 − 2) = $10

The pie is the largest amount of value that can be created—$10—and if competition is unrestricted, the connoisseur will buy the dark chocolate, and the lover will buy the milk chocolate.

For some intuition why this must be the case, imagine that the buyers are bidding for each firm's product. In the initial bidding, both buyers would be bidding only for their preferred choice: dark chocolate. The connoisseur would be willing to bid up to $8 for the dark chocolate. But consider the lover's situation: her willingness to pay for the dark chocolate is $10, so she could outbid the connoisseur if she wanted to. But this would never make any economic sense. Here is the reasoning: First, because the connoisseur will never bid for the milk chocolate, the lover always has the option to bid for (and win) the milk chocolate at an amount close to cost, namely $2. At this price, the lover would capture almost $4 (= 6 − 2) of value. As a result, any deal that the lover makes should give it a (buyer) profit of *at least $4*. Next, because the lover has a WTP of $10 for dark chocolate, and because the lover must get a profit of at least $4, she will not pay more than $6 to the dark-chocolate firm. Thus, we have a connoisseur willing to bid up to $8 for the dark chocolate, and a lover willing to bid up to $6. The connoisseur will outbid the lover and get the dark chocolate, and the lover will get the milk chocolate. This is exactly the outcome that maximizes the total value creation, as I noted above.

With that intuition as background, let's get back to guaranteed profitability. There may be more chocolate than buyers, but there is competition for the dark chocolate: both buyers are competing for it. The connoisseur has a willingness to pay of $8 for it, and as argued above, the lover is willing to pay up to $6 for it. Thus, from the perspective of the dark-chocolate firm, the lover acts like an excluded buyer with a willingness to pay of $6. Now the lover is not actually excluded—she will get milk chocolate—but she does provide a source of competition that acts like an excluded buyer.

Just as in the last chapter, a firm—the dark-chocolate firm—is guaranteed a profit due to competition from an outside buyer—the chocolate lover. But unlike the examples in the previous chapter, there is no excess demand in this story—every customer is served. However, the chocolate lover has been shut out from buying dark chocolate, and so she provides competitive pressure that benefits the dark-chocolate firm. As this example shows, even when every buyer is served, there can still be competition for a particular firm. And that competition will guarantee a profit for the firm.

In this example, the guaranteed profit is due to a guaranteed price of $6. But what is this $6? It is not the excluded buyer's willingness to pay—the chocolate lover's willingness to pay for dark chocolate is actually $10. In the story above, we saw that she would pay only up to $6 because of the possibility of buying milk chocolate. In what follows, I will describe, conceptually, the story that I told to determine the $6 figure.

Envious Buyers

If you look back at figure 7.1, you'll notice that the dark-chocolate firm has a value-gap advantage of $6 with respect to the connoisseur and $4 with respect to the lover. Because the firm could serve only one customer, it serves the one with whom it has the largest value-gap advantage. (This is another way to think about why the value creation is greatest with the dark-chocolate firm matched to the connoisseur and the milk-chocolate firm matched to the lover.) Even though the dark-chocolate firm is not serving the chocolate lover, its value gap with the lover is larger than the milk-chocolate firm's value gap with the lover. In other words, the dark-chocolate firm's value gap with a *competitor's* customer—the chocolate lover—is larger than the competitor's value gap with its own customer. When this occurs, we say that a firm has an *envious* buyer. To define such a buyer, consider a firm, and consider a customer of one of the firm's competitors:

If the competitor's value gap with the customer is less than the (hypothetical) value gap that the customer would have with the firm, then the customer is *envious* of the firm. Or, more simply, *if a firm has a value-gap advantage with respect to noncustomers, then it has envious buyers.*

Envy and Compensated WTP

An envious buyer is a source of competitive pressure, and it acts like an excluded buyer. But unlike an excluded buyer, it does have an option: transacting with a competing firm. Consequently, the competitive effect from an envious buyer's willingness to pay has to be reduced. In fact, it is reduced by the current buyer's existing value gap. *Game 7.1* illustrated the following fact:

Conditional on winning customers, a firm can always charge a price equal to the willingness to pay of another firm's buyer minus that buyer's value gap.

For this fact to be useful, we would want the firm's cost to be less than this price. If a buyer is envious, this will always be the case. Let's do the computation for our example. We'll start with the dark-chocolate firm's guaranteed price:

Envious buyer's (chocolate lover) WTP for dark-chocolate firm:	$10
Envious buyer's (chocolate lover) value gap:	– $4
Dark-chocolate firm's guaranteed price:	$6

Because $6 is greater than the dark chocolate firm's cost of $2, we have a guaranteed profit. How did we know that this price would be higher than the dark-chocolate firm's cost? Because the chocolate lover was envious. A little algebra makes this relationship more explicit.

Suppose that some firm's buyer is envious of another firm. Let's call this other firm "Other Firm." Then the definition of an envious buyer tells us that

$$\text{WTP}_{\text{Buyer}}(\text{Other Firm}) - \text{Cost}_{\text{Other Firm}} > \text{WTP}_{\text{Buyer}}(\text{Buyer's Firm}) - \text{Cost}_{\text{Buyer's Firm}}$$

In our example, the chocolate lover is envious of the dark-chocolate firm, so we write

$$\text{WTP}_{\text{lover}}(\text{Dark}) - \text{Cost}_{\text{Dark}} > \text{WTP}_{\text{lover}}(\text{Milk}) - \text{Cost}_{\text{Milk}}$$

This equation can be seen in the right-hand panel of figure 7.1: $10 - $2 > $6 - $2. Rearranging terms, the equation becomes

$$\text{WTP}_{\text{lover}}(\text{Dark}) - [\text{WTP}_{\text{lover}}(\text{Milk}) - \text{Cost}_{\text{Milk}}] > \text{Cost}_{\text{Dark}}$$

The left-hand side is the envious buyer's willingness to pay for the dark-chocolate firm minus the envious buyer's value gap with its own firm. As the equation demonstrates, this must be greater than the dark-chocolate firm's cost. In its general form, this equation becomes

$$\text{WTP}_{\text{Buyer}}(\text{Other Firm}) - [\text{WTP}_{\text{Buyer}}(\text{Buyer's Firm}) - \text{Cost}_{\text{Buyer's Firm}}] > \text{Cost}_{\text{Other Firm}}.$$

Before leaving this chapter, you might find it useful to review our two uses of value-gap advantages. In part II, you saw how you could win customers if you identified customer segments in which you had the largest value gap. And given our assumptions there, you learned how *potential* profitability was based on value-gap advantages with respect to your *customers*. In this chapter, we have seen how *guaranteed* profitability is based on value-gap advantages with respect to your *noncustomers*. Figure 7.2 annotates figure 7.1 with descriptions of the dark-chocolate firm's potential and guaranteed profit in terms of value-gap advantages.

To summarize our results from the last two chapters, it is convenient to come up with a term for "the willingness to pay of another firm's buyer minus that buyer's value gap." For any buyer of another firm's product, define that buyer's *compensated* willingness to pay for your firm as the willingness to pay (for your firm) minus the buyer's value gap with the other firm. In mathematical notation, a buyer's compensated WTP for another firm is the left-hand side of the equation we just derived above:

$$\text{WTP}_{\text{Buyer}}(\text{Your Firm}) - [\text{WTP}_{\text{Buyer}}(\text{Buyer's Firm}) - \text{Cost}_{\text{Buyer's Firm}}]$$

Note that if another firm's buyer has a compensated willingness to pay greater than your marginal cost, then that buyer is *envious*.

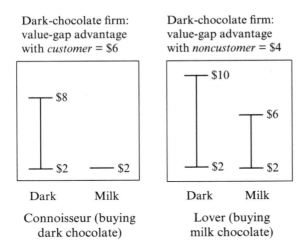

Figure 7.2
Potential and guaranteed profit for dark-chocolate firm

We can now summarize our results as follows:

Conditional on winning customers, a firm can always charge a price equal to either the willingness to pay of an excluded buyer or the compensated willingness to pay of another firm's buyer.

Excluded and envious buyers are the two main sources of guaranteed profitability, but they are not the only sources. In the next chapter we'll discuss how increasing marginal costs can guarantee profits to a firm.

8 Nonconstant Marginal Costs

So far, we have assumed that the cost of producing a product or service is constant. For a company that can make, say, 100 units of a product, we've assumed that the cost of the 100th unit is the same as the cost of the first. In economic terms, we have assumed that marginal costs are constant. There are some products for which this is a reasonable assumption—for instance, the cost of a handmade product is often constant. But the real reason for making this assumption was to keep things simple as we explored the importance of a firm's value creation with a buyer.

In this chapter, we'll relax the assumption and emphasize four consequences of doing so. The first is that with increasing marginal costs, a firm might be guaranteed a profit, even though there are no excluded or envious buyers. Second, by talking more generally about a firm's costs, I can provide a more general—and more precise—definition of a firm's value creation with a buyer. Third, a large increase in a firm's marginal cost can act like a capacity constraint. If you look back at the examples in chapter 7, you'll see that to get envious and excluded buyers, we limited the firm's capacity. In this chapter, you'll see that a jump in the marginal cost of a product can create envious and excluded buyers as well. And fourth, with nonconstant marginal costs, I will show that we can have instability in the competitive environment. It may be that the outcome of competition is completely unpredictable.

Increasing Marginal Costs and Guaranteed Profitability

We'll start with a slight variation of *Game 6.1*. *Game 8.1* still has one seller, ProScan, and four buyers, but in contrast to *Game 6.1*, we now assume that ProScan has four scanners, not three.

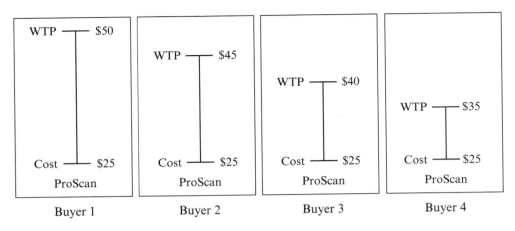

Figure 8.1
Game 8.1

With an additional scanner, the pie has now increased to $70 million dollars. There is no longer an excluded buyer, so it does not appear that ProScan has the power to set a price. My claim, though, is that ProScan has the power to set a price equal to its marginal cost. A firm's marginal cost is the cost of the last unit it provides. In this example, every unit has the same cost—$25—so this is also the marginal cost. Thus, ProScan can set a price of $25M, which guarantees it a profit of … zero.

At first glance, this result does not seem particularly interesting, as it merely says that a firm won't sell at a price below its cost. But let's see what happens with a different cost story. Suppose that ProScan can make two scanners for $20M each. Let's say that, in order to produce the third and fourth scanners, the firm has to start paying overtime, so that the third scanner would cost $22M and fourth scanner would cost $25M. Call this *Game 8.2*. It is often convenient to graph how a firm's unit cost changes as the production quantity changes. Figure 8.2 presents such a graph, and note that it is labeled with its formal name—the firm's *cost function*.

To figure out ProScan's marginal cost in this game, we need to first understand how many units it will provide. If it provides one or two units, the marginal cost is $20M. If it provides three units, the marginal cost is $22M. And if it provides four units, the marginal cost is $25M. Because the lowest WTP among the four buyers ($35M) is higher than the marginal cost of the fourth unit, we know that ProScan will be able to serve all four buyers and that its marginal cost will be $25M. Thus, ProScan can set a price of $25M, which guarantees it a profit of $13M. The fact that ProScan can set a price equal to its marginal cost now has some importance. It is true that ProScan

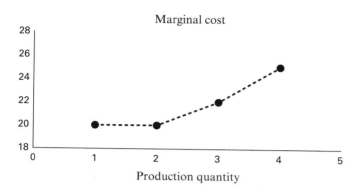

Figure 8.2
ProScan's cost function in *Game 8.2*

makes no money selling the fourth unit at this price—just as in *Game 8.1*—but it now makes $5M (= $25 − $20) on each of the first two units and $3M (=$25 − $22) on the third unit.

The Power to Set a Price Equal to Marginal Cost

Although it is clear that ProScan must get a price of at least $25M for the fourth unit, it is natural to ask why it is guaranteed to get that price for the other units. We can answer this question by using the fact that a player cannot receive more than it contributes. The pie is the value that ProScan creates with Buyers 1, 2, 3, and 4:

TVC = ($50M − $20M) + ($45M − $20M) + ($40M − $22M) + ($35M − $25M) = $83M

Consider what happens to the pie without, say, Buyer 2. The pie is reduced by Buyer 2's WTP, $45 million, but this is offset by ProScan's cost of serving Buyer 2, *on the margin*. In other words, without Buyer 2, ProScan would incur costs of $20M, $20M, and $22M in serving the other three buyers.

Pie w/o Buyer 2 = ($50M − $20M) + ($40M − $20M) + ($35M − $22M) = $63M

Thus, Buyer 2's contributed value is $20 million:

Buyer 2 ConV = $83M − $63M = $45M − $25M = $20M

Because Buyer 2 has a WTP of $45 million, this implies that the lowest price that Buyer 2 could pay is $25 million, which is ProScan's marginal cost. If we perform the same calculation for Buyers 1 and 3, we get the same answer—the lowest possible price is $25 million. ProScan is guaranteed this price with all four buyers.

Price-Setting Summary

I just showed that with unrestricted competition, a firm is guaranteed to receive a price equal to at least its marginal cost. We add this fact to our conclusions from chapter 7: *Conditional on winning customers, a firm can always charge a price equal to*

  its marginal cost, or

  the willingness to pay of an excluded buyer, or

  the compensated willingness to pay of another firm's buyer.

Given these facts, a firm's guaranteed price will be equal to at least the largest of these three categories. As it may not be immediately obvious which of these is the largest, here is a concrete procedure to determine the guaranteed price.

1. Consider all the buyers who are not transacting with your firm. Split them into two groups:

those buying from competitors

those not buying from anyone

2. Among those buying from competitors, take each buyer's willingness to pay for *your* firm and subtract out the buyer's value gap with the competitor's firm. Take whichever buyer gives the largest difference, and call this difference p_1. If p_1 is less than your marginal cost (this will happen if you don't have any envious buyers), set p_1 equal to your marginal cost.

3. Among those buyers not buying from anyone, assess which buyer has the largest willingness to pay for your firm's product, and call this willingness to pay p_2.

4. Whichever is larger, p_1 or p_2, is your firm's guaranteed price.

With this procedure, you actually get a conservative estimate. In the next chapter, you'll see how market-price effects can sometimes guarantee a price that is larger than the calculation above yields. Nonetheless, it is important to remember that, conceptually, guaranteed profits must ultimately rely on either marginal costs greater than average costs or buyer competition due to envious or excluded buyers.

Value Gap: A Firm's Marginal Value Creation with a Buyer

You might have noticed that I did not provide a new Rashomon diagram when I introduced *Game 8.2*. When a firm does not have constant marginal costs, we have to be careful about the number we use as the cost in our value gap. Because a firm can always charge a price equal to its marginal cost, you might suspect that we should use marginal cost in the value-gap calculation, and you would be correct. Recall that when I introduced value gaps, I said that they describe a firm's value creation with a customer. With nonconstant marginal costs, the description needs to be more precise. For a given customer, a value gap describes how much of the value the firm creates with the customer in question, assuming that the firm will serve all of its other customers. Thus, a firm's value gap with a customer is just its *marginal* value creation with that customer:

A firm's value gap with respect to a customer segment is equal to the WTP (of a buyer in the segment) minus the firm's marginal cost.

Note that this definition is consistent with what we have been doing all along, for if a firm has a constant cost per unit, then the cost per unit is the same as the marginal cost.

Marginal Cost as a Capacity Constraint

When marginal costs are no longer constant, a large enough jump in marginal cost can exclude buyers. If that happens, the effect can be the same as if the firm had no more capacity. *Game 8.3* demonstrates.

In *Game 8.3*, we have two firms, ProScan and TechScan. ProScan can make up to four scanners at a cost of $25 million each. If ProScan needs to make more scanners, it has to use a different manufacturing process, and any additional scanners will cost it $33 million per unit (see figure 8.3). TechScan can make as many scanners as needed at a cost of $20 million each. There is one segment of ten buyers, each of whom has a WTP of $50 million for a ProScan scanner and $40 million for a TechScan scanner.

For up to four buyers, ProScan will have a value-gap advantage of $5 million over TechScan, so it will clearly win these buyers. But what about the remaining six buyers? They will be TechScan's customers. A buyer can create $20 million with TechScan. But if ProScan is already serving four customers, the buyer can create only $17 million with ProScan. Thus, ProScan will serve four buyers, and TechScan will serve six.

In this example, there is excess supply—TechScan has no capacity limit. But is ProScan guaranteed a profit? Yes, because there are envious buyers. Any one of TechScan's six buyers would prefer to be one of the four ProScan buyers. Thus, ProScan is guaranteed a price of $50 million—[$40M – $20M] = $30 million: TechScan's compensated willingness to pay for ProScan's product. Because it will sell four units, ProScan is guaranteed a profit of $20 million.

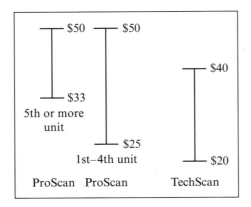

Figure 8.3
Game 8.3

The point to emphasize in this example is that if ProScan could produce only four units, the analysis would be the same. The increase in unit cost from $25 million to $33 million has the effect of limiting capacity. To appreciate the full effect of the phenomenon, it is important to realize that ProScan could feasibly deliver a fifth unit to a buyer: the buyer's WTP of $50 million exceeds the cost of $33 million. Thus, the effect of limiting capacity is not due to an increase in cost that makes production for a buyer infeasible. Rather, the increase in unit cost makes the extra units irrelevant from a competitive perspective. And when capacity is irrelevant from a competitive perspective, it might as well not exist.

Instability: The Dark Side of Economies of Scale

In *Games 8.1* through *8.3*, when the cost per unit changed, it increased as the firm produced more units. When this happens, a firm's average cost will increase as it produces more units. But sometimes a firm's average cost per unit goes *down* as it produces more units. In such cases, we can say that there is an *economy of scale* (or scale economy), where the term is almost self-explanatory. There is an economy—meaning the firm has lower costs—if it operates at a bigger scale—meaning if it produces at a higher volume.

In terms of competition, economies of scale have a positive and a negative aspect. On the positive side, economies of scale can lead to a cost advantage, but on the negative side, they can make competition highly unstable. Our main focus here is on the negative aspect, but let's look briefly at the positive first.

There are many different kinds of economy of scale, but for the insights we need, consider the case in which, to make a product, a firm has a fixed cost—say, the daily cost to operate a climate-controlled room—and then a constant cost per unit—say the costs of material and labor per unit. Let's say that a machine costs a firm a fixed cost of $45 per day, and each unit requires a total of $10 in material and labor per unit, for up to ten units per day. Further, let's suppose that the machine can make up to 15 units per day, and that the cost per unit rises steadily after ten units. (For instance, it might be that after ten units, the machine error rates start going up.) We'll suppose that the cost per unit rises by $2 per unit for units 11 through 15. For example, the marginal cost of the 12th unit will be $14. Figure 8.4 depicts the cost function for this example.

Figure 8.4 shows the average cost per unit, as well as the marginal cost per unit. (The lighter dotted line depicts the average cost per unit.) Note that if the company makes only one unit, its cost will be $55—$45 for the machine and $10 for the material and labor. But as the firm produces more units per day, its average cost decreases. This is the good news with an economy of scale: as the firm produces more, its average cost decreases, and as its average cost decreases, its profit per unit increases. This good news persists until the average cost starts rising. In figure 8.4, average cost decreases up to a production quantity of 12. As an aside, this quantity of 12 has a special name: minimum efficient scale. This is the point at which the firm's average cost per unit for the process is minimized.

But we have to be a little careful with this story—this is where the negative aspect of economy of scale comes in. Depending on the number of buyers, the effects of

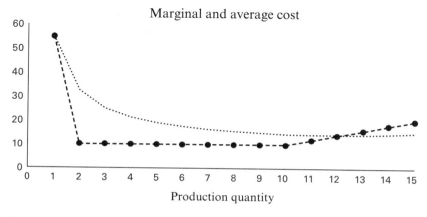

Figure 8.4
Economy of scale

competition can be quite different. To see this, suppose that we have two identical firms with the cost function depicted in figure 8.4. We'll consider three scenarios: one with over 30 buyers, one with 26 buyers, and one with only 20 buyers. We'll assume that the buyers are identical, with a willingness to pay of $30 for one unit.

1. With more than 30 buyers, there will be an excluded buyer, so we know that each firm is guaranteed a price of $30—the WTP of an excluded buyer.

2. With 26 buyers, all buyers will be served. There is excess supply, so buyers will not be competing for either firm. Nonetheless, each firm is guaranteed a profit due to the fact that a firm is always guaranteed a price of at least its marginal cost. With 26 buyers, each firm serves 13 buyers, and because the marginal cost of the 13th unit is greater than the average cost of 13 units, each firm is guaranteed a profit. By looking at figure 8.4, we can see that a firm is guaranteed a profit at 13 units because 13 is greater than minimum efficient scale, namely 12.

Whenever firms operate at or above minimum efficient scale, unrestricted competition will have predictable consequences. This is the case in scenarios 1 and 2, and we were able to apply our results from the previous chapters. Scenario 3 tells a different story.

3. With 20 buyers, all buyers again will be served. Which firm will serve them? Suppose that each firm serves ten. Note that a firm reduces its average cost by serving up to 12 buyers. So, if one firm competes successfully for two more buyers, there is now a 12–8 split of buyers between firms. But now the firm with eight buyers would have an incentive to compete for four more buyers. And so on. In any split of buyers between firms, at least one of the firms will have an incentive to compete for some of the other firm's buyers. The only insight from unrestricted competition is that the situation is *unstable*. The reason for the instability is that in the pie-maximizing scenario—each firm serving ten buyers—at least one of the firms has a marginal cost lower than the average cost.

The scenario with 20 buyers demonstrates the following insight:

When firms are operating at capacities in which average cost exceeds marginal cost, competition can be unstable.

This fact is familiar to anyone who has competed in a business in which the economies of scale do not "run out." With an economy of scale in a physical production process, there is typically a limit. (In figure 8.4 the limitations start with the 11th unit.) But sometimes an upfront, fixed investment can be spread over an almost unlimited number of buyers. (Think of some Internet, telecommunications, and media

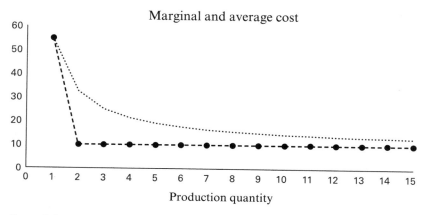

Figure 8.5
Unbounded economy of scale

companies.) When this is possible, there can be a financial bloodbath as firms fight for market share. Figure 8.5 provides the related cost function. The incentive to add buyers never runs outs, so the battle for market share is both necessary and unending.

As long as competition leads to a stable outcome, though, we know that a firm is guaranteed a price equal to at least its marginal cost, an excluded buyer's willingness to pay, or the willingness to pay of another firm's buyer minus that buyer's value gap. In the next chapter, we'll explore when a firm's guaranteed price can be even larger than these three numbers.

9 Market-Price Effects

In the previous three chapters, I showed that, conditional on winning customers, a firm can always charge a price equal to its marginal cost, the willingness to pay of an excluded buyer, or the compensated willingness to pay of another firm's buyer. If a firm's guaranteed price were always the largest of these three possibilities, we would have no more to discuss. But, as it turns out, there are circumstances under which a firm's guaranteed price will be larger than any of these three possibilities. This is due to what we'll call *market-price effects*.

There are two things you need to know about market-price effects. The first is that when they work in your favor, some firm—not necessarily yours—must have an envious or excluded buyer. Thus, the insights from the previous chapters will still be applicable. The second is that with market-price effects, there is typically no easy shortcut to determining a firm's guaranteed price. The advice to take the largest of marginal cost, an excluded buyer's willingness to pay, and the compensated willingness to pay of an envious buyer provides only a conservative estimate of a firm's guaranteed price. Determining how much higher the actual guaranteed price is often requires a more complicated calculation.

The Market-Price Intuition

To understand market-price effects, suppose that we have four segments of buyers looking for a place to live. One segment is interested in living only in an uptown apartment. A second segment would like to live in either an uptown apartment or a harborside apartment. A third segment would like to live in either a harborside apartment or a houseboat. And a fourth segment would like to live in either a houseboat or a trailer home.

Now, if there is excess demand for trailer homes, this will drive up prices for house-boats because the fourth segment will choose houseboats if trailers get too expensive. But the prices for houseboats could drive up the prices for harborside apartments because the third segment will choose harborside apartments if houseboats get too expensive. But if harborside apartments get too expensive, the second segment will start competing for uptown apartments. All of a sudden, the first segment will face higher prices for an uptown apartment. And the root cause for these increased prices will be the demand for trailers—even though there is not a single buyer who would view a trailer as an alternative to an uptown apartment!

This story might seem unrealistic, but the principle it demonstrates is not. This story exploits linkages in the preferences of different segments. Because of such linkages, demand for a seemingly unrelated product can affect your firm's guaranteed profit favorably. I'll provide a concrete example to go with the story above, but first let me identify the relationship that drives the effect.

The Market-Price Effect

Back in chapter 3, I noted that if a customer chose a product from company A at price $p(A)$ over a product from company B at price $p(B)$, then we would know that

$$\text{WTP}(A) - p(A) \geq \text{WTP}(B) - p(B)$$

We rearranged this equation in different ways to understand what price differences could tell us about differences in willingness to pay, and to understand how willing-ness-to-pay differences could affect prices. Here we rearrange this relationship in yet another way:

$$p(B) \geq \text{WTP}_{\text{A-Customer}}(B) - [\text{WTP}_{\text{A-Customer}}(A) - p(A)]$$

(I added a subscript to remind us that the willingnesses to pay in this example belong to a customer of Firm A.)

Since our interest is in a firm's guaranteed price, let $p^*(A)$ and $p^*(B)$ denote the guaranteed prices of Firms A and B, respectively. Then we have the following fact:

$$p^*(B) \geq \text{WTP}_{\text{A-Customer}}(B) - [\text{WTP}_{\text{A-Customer}}(A) - p^*(A)]$$

We call this relationship the *market-price effect*. It shows how the value capture of a noncustomer can affect a firm's guaranteed price. Figure 9.1 emphasizes this fact.

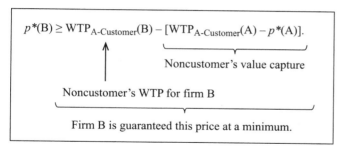

Figure 9.1
Market-price effect

Compensated Willingness to Pay, Revisited

With the introduction of market-price effects, we can explain why a noncustomer's compensated willingness to pay is a conservative estimate of a firm's guaranteed price. Keeping the same notation as above, the A-Customer's compensated willingness to pay for Firm B is

$$\text{WTP}_{\text{A-Customer}}(B) - [\text{WTP}_{\text{A-Customer}}(A) - \text{Cost}(A)]$$

where Cost(A) is Firm A's marginal cost. We saw in chapter 8 that this implied the following:

$$p^*(B) \geq \text{WTP}_{\text{A-Customer}}(B) - [\text{WTP}_{\text{A-Customer}}(A) - \text{Cost}(A)]$$

If we contrast this equation with the equation in figure 9.1, we see that they are identical if $p^*(A) = \text{Cost}(A)$—namely, if Firm A's guaranteed price is just its marginal cost.

Recall that the expression $[\text{WTP}_{\text{A-Customer}}(A) - \text{Cost}(A)]$ is the marginal value that the A-Customer creates with Firm A. Consequently, it is the maximum value that the A-Customer could capture. But if Firm A is guaranteed a price above its marginal cost— if $p^*(A) > \text{Cost}(A)$—then the A-Customer could capture, at most, $\text{WTP}_{\text{A-Customer}}(A) - p^*(A)$. This benefits Firm B, as the "compensation" to $\text{WTP}_{\text{ACustomer}}(B)$ is now smaller. The compensating term has been reduced from $[\text{WTP}_{\text{A-Customer}}(A) - \text{Cost}(A)]$ to $[\text{WTP}_{\text{A-Customer}}(A) - p^*(A)]$. This is the essence of the market-price effect.

To summarize, a noncustomer's compensated willingness to pay may underestimate a firm's guaranteed price because it assumes that the noncustomer's firm is guaranteed only a price equal to its marginal cost.

Market-Price Effects Creating Envious Buyers

The equation in figure 9.1 shows how guaranteed prices must be related, and this is one way to understand how market-price effects can benefit firms. But one can also think of market-price effects benefiting firms by creating envious buyers.

Recall that if a customer of Firm A were envious of Firm B, it could create more value with Firm B than it would capture with Firm A. Continuing with the notation from above, we write this as

$$\text{WTP}_{\text{A-Customer}}(B) - \text{Cost}(B) > \text{WTP}_{\text{A-Customer}}(A) - \text{Cost}(A)$$

Now suppose that some customer of firm A is not envious of firm B, so that we have

$$\text{WTP}_{\text{A-Customer}}(B) - \text{Cost}(B) < \text{WTP}_{\text{A-Customer}}(A) - \text{Cost}(A)$$

But suppose that we also have a market-price effect, and Firm B is guaranteed a price above its marginal cost. Then we would have

$$\text{WTP}_{\text{A-Customer}}(B) - [\text{WTP}_{\text{A-Customer}}(A) - p^*(A)] > \text{Cost}(B)$$

Rearranging this last equation, we have

$$\text{WTP}_{\text{A-Customer}}(B) - \text{Cost}(B) > \text{WTP}_{\text{A-Customer}}(A) - p^*(A)$$

In words, we have an envious buyer story again. Firm A's customer is envious of Firm B because it can create more value with Firm B than it can capture with Firm A. Because Firm A is guaranteed a price above its marginal cost, Firm A's customer cannot capture $\text{WTP}_{\text{A-Customer}}(A) - \text{Cost}(A)$. Instead, it can capture only $\text{WTP}_{\text{A-Customer}}(A) - p^*(A)$. And because

$$\text{WTP}_{\text{A-Customer}}(B) - \text{Cost}(B) > \text{WTP}_{\text{A-Customer}}(A) - p^*(A)$$

we can say that *market-price effects have created an envious buyer*. The customer of Firm A has been made envious of Firm B due to the fact that Firm A is guaranteed a price above marginal cost.

If a firm is benefiting from a market-price effect, then we can always identify a noncustomer who has been made envious by the market-price effect. This perspective provides a useful way to summarize the three reasons that a firm might be guaranteed a price above its marginal cost. It might have an excluded buyer, it might have an envious buyer, or it might have a buyer made envious by a market-price effect.

An Example

Let's see an example of how market-price effects work. Game *9.1* has five buyers and four sellers. Each of the sellers has just one "apartment" to sell, and each of the buyers is interested in buying just one apartment. The buyers have different tastes, so technically we have five buyer segments of one buyer each. Figure 9.2 depicts the segments. To save space, for each segment, I show only the value gaps for apartments for which the buyer has a positive willingness to pay. For instance, Buyer 1 is interested only in an uptown apartment, and Buyer 3 is interested only in a harborside apartment or a houseboat. The figure also leaves out the cost numbers (for visual simplicity). The dotted horizontal lines depict each seller's guaranteed price. I'll explain them now.

To start, note that Buyer 5 is excluded, so the trailer owner is guaranteed Buyer 5's willingness to pay for a trailer—$80 thousand. So we can write

p^*(Trailer) = $80

At the beginning of this chapter, I said that for market-price effects to work in your favor, some firm—not necessarily yours—must have an envious or excluded buyer. In this example, the trailer owner is the firm with the envious or excluded buyer—Buyer 5. Because of market-price effects, we will see how the trailer owner's guaranteed price affects the other owners.

Consider Buyer 4. Because the trailer owner is guaranteed a price of $80 thousand, Buyer 4 will capture, at most, $20 thousand when buying a trailer. Given this fact, if houseboat prices drop below $80 thousand, then Buyer 4 is a legitimate buyer for a houseboat. So the houseboat owner can get a price of at least $80 thousand in its

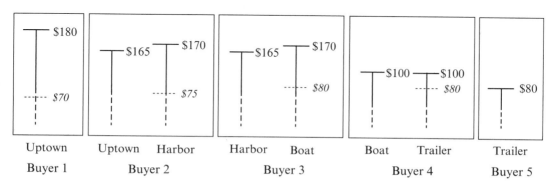

Figure 9.2
Game 9.1

transaction with Buyer 3. We've just described a market-price effect, and it can be stated mathematically as

$$p^*(\text{Boat}) \geq \text{WTP}_{\text{Buyer 4}}(\text{Boat}) - [\text{WTP}_{\text{Buyer 4}}(\text{Trailer}) - p^*(\text{Trailer})]$$
$$= \$100 - [\$100 - \$80] = \$80$$

We can keep going. Buyer 3 will capture, at most, $90 thousand when buying a houseboat. Given this fact, he would be willing to pay up to $75 thousand for a harborside apartment. So the harborside apartment owner can get a price of at least $75 thousand in its transaction with Buyer 2. Mathematically,

$$p^*(\text{Harbor}) \geq \text{WTP}_{\text{Buyer 3}}(\text{Harbor}) - [\text{WTP}_{\text{Buyer 3}}(\text{Boat}) - p^*(\text{Boat})]$$
$$= \$165 - [\$170 - \$80] = \$75$$

Finally, Buyer 2 will capture, at most, $95 thousand when buying a harborside apartment. Given this fact, he would be willing to pay up to $70 thousand for an uptown apartment. So the uptown apartment owner can get a price of at least $70 thousand in its transaction with Buyer 1:

$$p^*(\text{Uptown}) \geq \text{WTP}_{\text{Buyer 2}}(\text{Uptown}) - [\text{WTP}_{\text{Buyer 2}}(\text{Harbor}) - p^*(\text{Harbor})]$$
$$= \$165 - [\$170 - \$75] = \$70$$

In this example, it is important to remember the reason that the uptown apartment owner is guaranteed a price of at least $70 thousand in its transaction with Buyer 1: excess demand for a trailer home. Trailer homes and uptown apartments might never directly compete with each other, but due to market-price effects, competition for one can affect the other. Identifying these effects can often involve several segments, and that is why I noted, at the start of this chapter, that there is typically no easy shortcut to determining a firm's guaranteed price. For instance, if you wanted to describe the uptown owner's guaranteed price in terms of its competitive "source"—namely the trailer owner's guaranteed price—you would have the following formula:

$$p^*(\text{Uptown}) \geq \text{WTP}_{\text{Buyer 2}}(\text{Uptown}) - \text{WTP}_{\text{Buyer 2}}(\text{Harbor})$$
$$+ \text{WTP}_{\text{Buyer 3}}(\text{Harbor}) - \text{WTP}_{\text{Buyer 3}}(\text{Boat})$$
$$+ \text{WTP}_{\text{Buyer 4}}(\text{Boat}) - \text{WTP}_{\text{Buyer 4}}(\text{Trailer}) + p^*(\text{Trailer})$$

If you prefer, you can actually provide a verbal description that approximates this equation: "Buyer 4 views houseboats and trailers as equivalent. Buyer 3 believes that a harborside apartment is $5 thousand worse than a houseboat. Buyer 2 believes an uptown apartment is $5 thousand worse than a houseboat. Thus, the market price for an uptown apartment should be $10 thousand less than the market price for a trailer."

This description is not quite precise—it glosses over the critical issue of who will buy what—but it does capture the intuition of the result.

Given the potential complexity of market-price effects, how should you think about a firm's guaranteed price? My advice is to start with our conservative estimate: a firm's guaranteed price will be the greatest of its marginal cost, the largest willingness to pay among excluded buyers, and the largest compensated willingness to pay among envious buyers. Then, be aware that if some competing firm is guaranteed a price above its marginal cost, this could create buyers that are effectively envious of your firm.

More generally, it is useful to remember that market-price effects arise due to linkages in buyer preferences (in the example above, Buyer 1 liking uptown and harborside apartments, Buyer 2 liking harborside apartments and houseboats, etc.). Furthermore, people often implicitly assume that these linkages exist. For instance, people often talk about "the" housing market going up or down when in fact there are many different housing markets. But as our example shows, due to linkages in buyer preferences, movements in prices across different markets can be related. Thus, treating these markets as a whole can provide a reasonable overview.

10 Being in Demand: Guaranteed and Potential Profitability

In chapters 6 through 9, we explored the impact of nonconstant marginal costs on guaranteed profitability. Increasing marginal costs can act like a capacity constraint, and with capacity constraints, we can have exclusion. And with exclusion, a firm can be in demand. So far, we have looked at how exclusion can create competition that guarantees your firm a profit. But exclusion can also improve a firm's potential profit. Relatedly, and perhaps more important, exclusion can allow a firm without value-gap advantages to also be profitable. Consequently, exclusion will be the rationale behind the advice to be in demand if you cannot be better. In this chapter, we'll look at the impact of exclusion on both potential profitability and the profitability of firms without value-gap advantages. As a starting point, we consider a benchmark situation in which firms have nonconstant marginal costs, but in which there is no exclusion.

A Useful Benchmark

To isolate the effects of exclusion from the effects of nonconstant marginal costs, consider situations in which each firm has extra capacity at its marginal cost. In other words, each firm can produce at least one more unit at its marginal cost. Additionally, each firm's marginal cost must be greater than or equal to its average cost. This is to ensure that competition will lead to a stable outcome. (See the discussion near the end of chapter 8.) Given these two conditions, if competition is unrestricted, and if a given firm has segments in which it has the largest value gap, then

1. that firm is guaranteed a price equal to its marginal cost, and
2. that firm's potential profit is equal to the sum of its value-gap advantages plus any profits guaranteed by a price equal to marginal cost.

(As discussed in part II of this book, a firm's value-gap advantage with a buyer is computed with respect to whichever firm has the next-largest value gap with the buyer.)

If every firm has constant marginal costs, this benchmark result reduces to the result at the end of chapter 5: to be profitable, a firm must identify customer segments in which it has the largest value gap. With constant marginal costs, a price equal to marginal cost will guarantee a firm a profit of zero. Thus, a firm's only source of profit comes from capturing its potential profit, and to have potential profit in this situation, it must have value-gap advantages.

Without constant marginal costs, note that, conditional on winning customers, there is an additional source of guaranteed profit: profits due to marginal cost exceeding average cost. We saw an example of this guaranteed profit in *Game 8.2*. ProScan had four scanners for four buyers, so it was not guaranteed any profits due to exclusion. But it had costs of $20 million for each of its first two units, $22 million for the third unit, and $25 million for the fourth. Because it was guaranteed a price equal to its marginal cost, it was guaranteed a profit of $13 million. Alternatively, its average cost per unit was $21.75 million, $3.25 million less than its marginal cost. Multiplying by the four units, we again have the guaranteed profit of $13 million.

When such profits exist, they must also increase the firm's potential profit. Thus, in the benchmark result above, potential profits include both value-gap advantages and profit from marginal cost exceeding average cost.

This benchmark result gives us baselines for guaranteed and potential profit with nonconstant marginal costs, but without the effects of exclusion. Thus, any improvements to these baselines will identify the effects of exclusion. In chapters 6, 7, and 9, you saw how exclusion could guarantee a firm a price above its marginal cost. With excluded buyers, envious buyers, or envious buyers created by market-price effects, a firm could be guaranteed a price above its marginal cost. What is the equivalent result for a firm's potential profit? In particular, how can exclusion—being in demand—increase a firm's potential profit above the sum of its value-gap advantages? I'll address these questions next.

Potential Profit and Exclusion

In the benchmark result above—and in the result at the end of chapter 5—a firm's value-gap advantage is based on its advantage over the firm with the next-largest value gap. If this next-best firm has an extra unit of capacity at its marginal cost, this extra unit of capacity is a next-best option for your customer. This is the intuition behind value-gap advantages, as we saw in part II. But what if the next-best firm can't supply an extra unit, or what if the next-best firm's incremental cost of an extra unit is much larger than its marginal cost? Then the value gap of the next-best firm does not provide your customer with a viable option. And, as a result, you have the potential to capture even more value. This explains why exclusion can improve a firm's potential profit. Let's see how it works in an example.

In *Game 10.1*, we have four firms, each with the capacity to produce just one unit. The firms have an identical product but different costs for making the product. There is one segment of just three buyers, each with a willingness to pay of $50 million for just one unit of the product. Figure 10.1 depicts the situation.

Before analyzing this game, suppose that Firm B had no capacity constraints. One buyer would transact with Firm A, and two buyers would transact with Firm B. Firm A's potential profit would be based on its value-gap advantage over Firm B—namely $5 million. Firm B would still have extra capacity, so it would be a source of competition for Firm A's customer. Note that Firm A's capacity constraint does not improve its *potential* profit. (We can easily verify that it does improve its guaranteed profit; see chapter 7.)

Now consider *Game 10.1*. Firm B does not have an extra unit of capacity, so it won't be a source of competition for Firm A. In fact, the only firm with extra capacity is Firm D, so we might suspect that Firm A's potential profit would be based on its advantage over Firm D rather than over Firm B. In this example, that is the case. Firm A's potential profit is $15 million—based on its advantage over Firm D: [$50M – $25M] – [$50M – $40M]. This is considerably more than its value-gap advantage in the buyer segment—$5 million. *Game 10.1* illustrates the following key point. For capacity

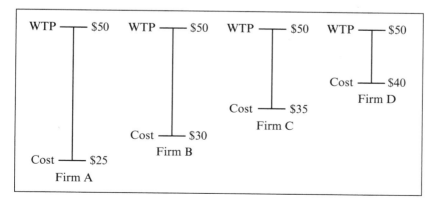

Figure 10.1
Game 10.1

constraints to increase a firm's potential profit, the alternative for the firm's buyers must be constrained. In other words, there must also be exclusion affecting the firm with the next-largest value gap.

For the intuition behind this point, remember why a firm's potential profit is based on its value-gap advantages, rather than on just its value gaps with its buyers. A firm's value gap with one of its buyers is its marginal value creation with this buyer. The reason that the firm cannot capture potentially all of this value creation is that the buyer typically has an alternative—the firm with which the buyer has the next-largest value gap. Thus, the firm's potential profit is limited to its advantage over the buyer's next-best alternative. In *Game 10.1*, the buyer's next-best alternative is taken, as it were. In fact, Firm A's buyer's best *available* alternative is its third-best alternative, Firm D.

Be in Demand

Game 10.1 shows that if some firms are constrained, a particular firm does not necessarily need to have buyer segments in which it has the largest value gap. Neither Firm B nor Firm C has a value-gap advantage, but they both have the potential for profits. There is excess demand for Firm A, and Firms B and C benefit. This illustrates the advice to "be in demand" if your firm is not "better"—that is, if your firm does not have buyer segments in which it has the largest value gap. And because Firms B and C have an advantage over Firm D, they benefit from the excess demand for Firm A: Firm B has a potential profit of $10 million, and Firm C has a potential profit of $5 million.

In the appendix to chapter 6, I use contributed value to show how games like *Game 10.1* capture traditional supply-and-demand reasoning. In the appendix to this chapter, I use the results from chapters 6, 7, and 9 and the current chapter to show how supply-and-demand reasoning can be understood in terms of guaranteed and potential profit.

Potential Profit and Market-Price Effects

Based on Game *10.1*, it might seem that we could derive a general result for potential profitability by generalizing the definition of a value-gap advantage. Rather than looking at your firm's value-gap advantage over the firm with the next-largest value gap, you would look at your firm's value-gap advantage over the firm with the next-largest value gap of available capacity. Conceptually, this is the right idea, but in practice, this rule does not always work. The reason is that the notion of "available capacity" has to be adjusted for market-price effects. *Game 10.2* demonstrates the issue. To derive *Game 10.2*, I changed the preferences of the four buyers in *Game 10.1*. Buyer 1 is interested only in Firm A's or Firm B's product, Buyer 2 only in Firm B's or Firm C's product, and Buyer 3 only in Firm C's or Firm D's product; see figure 10.2.

In *Game 10.2*, each firm's guaranteed and potential profits are the same as in *Game 10.1*. Firm A still has a value-gap advantage of $5 million in its buyer segment, but consider its advantage over the next available unit of capacity. Firm D has the only extra capacity, and Buyer 1 has zero willingness to pay for Firm D. So Firm A's value-gap advantage over Firm D is its full value-gap—namely $25 million. But Firm A's potential profit is still $15 million. Why? Because of market-price effects.

In chapter 9, we explored how market-price effects could improve a firm's guaranteed profit. In the current game, market-price effects improve the *buyers'* guaranteed profit. This then limits the firms' potential profits. Here is a verbal description of the logic: Because of Firm D's extra capacity, Firm C's potential profit is limited. As a result, Firm C would be happy to serve Buyer 2 rather than Buyer 3, *at the right price*. Because Firm C would be happy to serve Buyer 2 at the right price, this limits Firm B's potential profit. As a result, Firm B would be happy to serve Buyer 1 rather than Buyer 2, *at the right price*. In short, because of market-price effects, there is a price at which Firm B provides an alternative for Buyer 1.

Let's put these words into equations. Buyer 3 is guaranteed a profit of $10 million due to Firm D's extra capacity. Given that Buyer 3's WTP for Firm C is $50 million, a

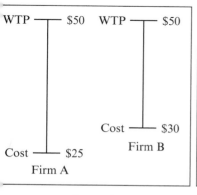 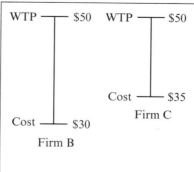 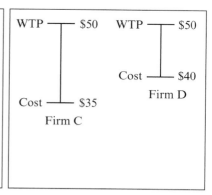

Buyer 1   Buyer 2   Buyer 3

Figure 10.2
Game 10.2

guaranteed buyer profit of $10 million implies a maximum price of $40 million for Firm C. If we let $p^{\max}(C)$ denote the maximum price that Firm C can receive, we have

$p^{\max}(C) \leq \$40$ million

As in chapter 9, we exploit market-price effects. The relationships are the same, except that now we use a firm's maximum price rather than its guaranteed price. Thus, we know that

$p^{\max}(C) \geq \text{WTP}_{\text{Buyer 2}}(C) - [\text{WTP}_{\text{Buyer 2}}(B) - p^{\max}(B)]$

$p^{\max}(B) \geq \text{WTP}_{\text{Buyer 1}}(B) - [\text{WTP}_{\text{Buyer 1}}(A) - p^{\max}(A)]$

Because of the buyer preferences in this game, these equations simplify to

$p^{\max}(C) \geq p^{\max}(B)$

$p^{\max}(B) \geq p^{\max}(A)$

so no firm can get a price above $40 million. In particular, Firm B will not get a price above $40 million. Consequently, Firm B is a viable alternative for Buyer 1, provided that Buyer 1 is willing to pay at least $40 million. Let's now look at Firm A's value-gap advantage over Firm B with respect to Buyer 1, with the restriction that Buyer 1 would not pay more than $40 million to Firm B:

$[\text{WTP}_{\text{Buyer 1}}(A) - \text{Cost}(A)] - [\text{WTP}_{\text{Buyer 1}}(B) - p^{\max}(B)]$

$[\$50M - \$25M] - [\$50M - \$40M] = \$15$ million.

We are left with Firm A's potential profit, as claimed just above. More generally, we see that potential profits are based on value-gap advantages, provided that we use a market-price-adjusted maximum price for the buyer's next-best alternative. The problem, of course, is that with capacity constraints, there is no easy way to determine the market-price-adjusted maximum price.

Potential Profitability—The General Case

Similar to the question at the end of chapter 9, given the potential complexity of market-price effects, how should you think about a firm's potential profitability? My answer follows the narrative of this chapter. Starting with the benchmark result, we have the *minimum* estimate of a firm's potential profit: a firm's value-gap advantages, plus any profits due to marginal cost exceeding average cost. Based on *Game 10.1*, we have the *maximum* estimate: a firm's value-gap advantages, defined with respect to the next-largest value gap of available capacity, plus any profits due to marginal cost exceeding average cost. Note that, in general, this maximum will not be achievable. Finally, based on *Game 10.2*, we have the *actual* potential profit: a firm's value-gap advantages, defined with respect to the market-price-adjusted, next-largest value gap of available capacity, plus any profits due to marginal cost exceeding average cost. Of course, this last definition takes all the complexities of market-price effects and lumps them into the phrase "market-price adjusted." But as with guaranteed profits, the important point is that there can be linkages in buyer preferences. And because of these linkages, your firm's advantage over a firm with available capacity might be reduced.

Being in Demand, Revisited

Without linkages in buyer preferences, we have a simple rule-of-thumb for an "inferior" firm to have potential profitability: Have a value-gap advantage over the next-available unit of capacity. With linkages in buyer preferences, this rule provides an initial assessment of whether profitability is even feasible. But you will have to then assess the impact of the linkages.

Appendix: Supply and Demand Revisited

In the appendix to chapter 6, I used contributed values to derive the traditional supply and demand results. In this appendix, we will see how these traditional results also can be derived using market-price effects.

In *Game 10.1* each buyer's willingness-to-pay does not depend on which firm it transacts with, and each firm's cost does not depend on which buyer it sells to, so we can depict the game with supply and demand curves as in figure 10.3.

The thick, gray line depicts the intersection of the supply and demand curves. The highest point of this intersection corresponds to a price of $40 million. This price determines the potential profit of each firm. The lowest point of the intersection corresponds to $35 million. This price determines the guaranteed profit of each firm. We'll consider the latter price first.

Guaranteed Price

Label the firms A through D, with A corresponding to the firm with the lowest cost and D corresponding to the firm with the highest cost. Firm C will not transact at a price below its cost, so we start with

$p^*(C) = \$35$ million

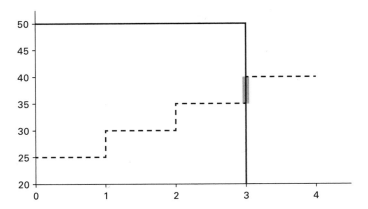

Figure 10.3
Supply-and-demand picture for *Game 10.1*

Recall the equation for the relationship between guaranteed prices:

$p*(B) \geq WTP_{C\text{-Customer}}(B) - [WTP_{C\text{-Customer}}(C) - p*(C)]$

$p*(A) \geq WTP_{C\text{-Customer}}(A) - [WTP_{C\text{-Customer}}(C) - p*(C)]$

Because a buyer's willingness to pay does not depend on which firm it buys from, these equations reduce to

$p*(B) \geq p*(C) = \$35$ million

$p*(A) \geq p*(C) = \$35$ million

Firms A, B, and C are guaranteed a price of at least \$35 million, as we needed to show.

To interpret this guaranteed price, start with Firm C. It has neither an excluded nor an envious buyer, so it is guaranteed its marginal cost, \$35 million. But what about Firms A and B? Our equations show that they are guaranteed a price above marginal cost, but where is the envious or the excluded buyer? It is Firm C's buyer. Because each buyer has the same WTP for all firms, it might be hard to identify the "envy," but it is there. The value created with Firm C and a buyer is \$35 million. The value created with Firm A or B is greater. So whichever buyer transacts with Firm C will be envious of both Firm A and Firm B.

Potential Price

Firm D is excluded, so its maximum price must be its cost:

$p^{\max}(D) = \$40$ million

Using market-price effects, we have

$$p^{max}(D) \geq WTP_{C\text{-}Customer}(D) - [WTP_{C\text{-}Customer}(C) - p^{max}(C)]$$

$$p^{max}(D) \geq WTP_{B\text{-}Customer}(D) - [WTP_{B\text{-}Customer}(B) - p^{max}(B)]$$

$$p^{max}(D) \geq WTP_{A\text{-}Customer}(D) - [WTP_{A\text{-}Customer}(A) - p^{max}(A)]$$

Because of the buyer preferences in this game, these equations simplify to

$$p^{max}(D) \geq p^{max}(C)$$

$$p^{max}(D) \geq p^{max}(B)$$

$$p^{max}(D) \geq p^{max}(A)$$

so no firm can get a price above $40 million, as we needed to show.

To interpret this potential price, note that each firm's potential profit is just its value-gap advantage over Firm D. For instance, Firm B's value-gap advantage over Firm D is

$$[WTP_{B\text{-}Customer}(B) - Cost(B)] - [WTP_{B\text{-}Customer}(D) - Cost(D)]$$

which equals $10 million. A profit of $10 million for Firm B implies a price of $40 million—that is, the potential price.

11   Profitability under Unrestricted Competition

When firms have constant marginal costs, the advice for achieving profitability is succinct, provided that competition is unrestricted: find buyer segments in which you have a value-gap advantage. With the possibility of increasing marginal costs and capacity constraints, this advice still applies, but it is no longer necessary. Due to the possibility of market-price effects, there is no simple way to refine this advice for more general cost functions. Instead, consider the following advice for potential profitability distilled from parts II and III of this book:

Find buyer segments in which you have a value-gap advantage.

This advice is the most robust. As long as your firm can identify segments in which it has a value-gap advantage, it will have the potential for profitability. Moreover, your potential profitability will always be equal to *at least* the sum of your firm's value-gap advantages. Business strategists tend to be a pessimistic group. In particular, they always believe that there will be competition for your products. For them, this first piece of advice is the essential piece. But there certainly are profitable firms without value-gap advantages, so let's move on to the second piece of advice:

Find buyer segments in which there is excess demand for any "better" firms, and in which you have a value-gap advantage over the buyers' next-best available alternative.

This advice, based on the insights from chapter 10, is not as concise. If any firm with a larger value gap than yours is at capacity, and if demand in the buyer segment has not been met, then there is the potential for profitability. Value-gap reasoning is still applicable, though—your firm's value gap has to be larger than that of firms with available capacity. And you have to be aware that when computing the *size* of your value-gap advantage, you need to consider the market-price-adjusted value gaps of firms at capacity in addition to the value gaps of firms with available capacity.

Finally, there is the limiting case in which you are the worst firm that can serve a buyer segment, but due to excess demand, you will have customers. This is a limiting case because your firm is still better than the next-best alternative, which is no alternative for the buyer. This is the classic case of "being on the right side of the market," but it is a precarious case. Entry by a more capable competitor, much less expansion by an existing competitor, would eliminate your firm's profitability in this scenario.

Guaranteed Profitability

Conditional on having potential profits, there are two sources of guaranteed profitability: marginal costs exceeding average costs and exclusion. Any advice to improve guaranteed profitability will typically adversely affect potential profits. Creating exclusion usually implies underserving your customer base. Increasing your marginal cost will decrease your value gap, and hence your value-gap advantage. So rather than provide advice, I reiterate that exclusion takes three forms:

Unserved buyers   A firm is always guaranteed a price equal to the willingness to pay of an unserved buyer.

Envious buyers   A firm is always guaranteed a price equal to the compensated willingness to pay of another firm's buyer, where the compensation equals the buyer's value gap with the other firm.

Market-price-induced envious buyers   A firm is always guaranteed a price equal to the compensated willingness to pay of another firm's buyer, where the compensation equals the buyer's maximum value capture with the other firm.

Potential and Guaranteed Profitability: An Informal Summary

The advice for potential profitability can be summarized loosely as "be needed"—in a value-creating sense. Whether your firm is the "best" firm for your customers or just the best available firm, your firm is needed for value creation. The advice for guaranteed profitability can be summarized as "be competed for." Thus, an informal, but useful, summary of our results is simply: to be profitable, be needed for value creation; to be guaranteed those profits, have competition for your firm.

IV Your Firm's Game

12 Buyers and Competitors

In parts II and III, we covered the economic theory for thinking about a firm's profitability when competition is unrestricted. I used stylized games to introduce and demonstrate the main ideas. Stylized games are useful because you can design them to illustrate specific points while excluding confounding factors. But when considering the profitability of a real-world business—your business—we cannot rely on a stylized game. Instead, we must construct a game that captures the essence of *your firm's* strategic situation.

As noted in chapter 2, there are two elements to a business game—the players and the potential value that any group of players can create. To construct a game for a particular firm, you need to first identify the players that are relevant to that firm. Having identified the relevant players, you can then determine potential value creation for any group of players, provided that you have some idea about willingnesses to pay and costs. In part I, I discussed some of the issues involved in determining willingnesses to pay and costs. In part IV, I'll address the question of which players to include in the game.

Although determining willingnesses to pay and costs might seem like a difficult task, deciding which players to include in the game can be even harder. The business world is an interconnected world, so you can often make an argument for including many, many players in a game. But with too many players, the game becomes huge, and the analysis of the game gets overly complicated. In this part of the book, you'll see that choosing the players to include in a game involves both art and science. In these next chapters, I'll provide insight into both, starting with the most basic players—buyers and competitors.

Buyers

In the broadest sense, you could say that everyone is potentially a buyer, but such a broad criterion for being a buyer would clearly not help us define a meaningful game. Instead, we start with the firm whose profitability interests us—let's call it *your firm*. A buyer is relevant—meaning should be in your game—if it perceives your firm to be a producer of the good or service it might pay for, and if its willingness to pay exceeds your marginal cost. If a buyer meets these two criteria, it should be included in your game. To be clear, a buyer should be included in your game if

1. the buyer knows about your firm (or can be made to know about your firm), and

2. the buyer has a willingness-to-pay for your firm that exceeds your marginal cost.

(As an aside, if a buyer does not know about your firm, or if it would never consider buying from your firm, then it has zero willingness to pay for your firm's product. So, by assigning a positive willingness to pay to a buyer, you are assuming that the buyer both knows about your product and would purchase it if it gave the buyer the greatest value capture.)

Note that these two criteria cover the buyers that one would naturally think of: both current and potential customers, whether they are unserved or served by competitors. But there are other buyers that also should be in the game. For instance, recall *Game 9.1*, which is displayed again in figure 12.1. Suppose that you own the uptown apartment and are trying to construct a game to understand your profitability.

For the uptown owner, there are only two buyers—Buyers 1 and 2—that meet the criteria for being included in the game. Yet, if you recall the analysis of *Game 9.1*,

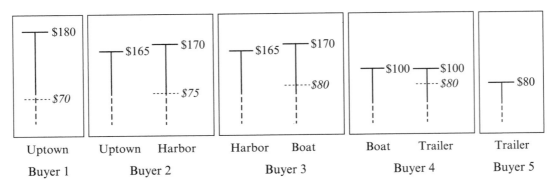

Figure 12.1
Game 9.1

Buyer 5—the excluded buyer of a trailer home—positively affected the profits of the uptown apartment owner. So clearly, as the uptown apartment owner, when you construct the game, you need to include Buyer 5, even though Buyer 5 has no interest in your apartment. To show you how a buyer like Buyer 5 can be relevant to your firm, I first need to talk about competitors.

Competitors

In many cases, it may seem obvious who your competitors are, but for the purposes of determining firm profitability, there are two criteria for including a competitor in your game. A competing firm should be included in your game if

1. some of your buyers would consider doing business with it, *and*
2. it will react to your pricing decisions (i.e., they see you as a competitor).

Note an interesting aspect of this definition: *you* do not define who your competitors are. Rather, your buyers and your competitors do. Start with the buyers. You might be concerned about a firm that has a competing product, but if none of your buyers would think of buying the competing product, then the competing product is not relevant to you.

Now consider a possible competitor. If your buyers view another firm's product as a viable alternative, isn't that firm a competitor, whether or not it will react to your pricing decisions? If the firm won't react to you, then the answer is "no." The firm is important, but it is not a competitor. This might seem counterintuitive, but it will make sense if we revisit our definition of a buyer's willingness to pay.

Recall that when I defined a buyer's willingness to pay in chapter 3, I always computed it with respect to a fixed outside option. In other words, I based the calculation on an option that was "out of the game." A firm that has a competing product but that will not react to you is such an option. Because it will not react to you, you leave it out of the game. But if a buyer views that firm's product as an alternative, then the firm—though not in the game—will be important because it provides the fixed outside option.

Let's look at a simple example. Suppose that your company runs a discount bus service between Boston and New York. The kind of buyer that would consider taking your bus will also consider taking an established bus service or the train. You know that the established bus services will react to you if necessary, but you believe that the train service will not. The train company will keep its ticket prices fixed no matter how you price your bus service. In this scenario, the train company is out of the game, and a buyer's willingnesses to pay for your bus service and the established bus service will use the ticket price of the train as the fixed outside option.

Alternatively, if you believe that the train company will react to you, then the train company is a competitor in the game. And a buyer's willingness to pay for your bus service, the established bus service, and the train will be based on some other outside option, say renting a car, flying, or, perhaps, the "cost" of not traveling at all.

A competitor in your game, then, must be seen as a competitor by your buyers *and* must view your firm as a competitor. This is the sense in which your buyers and your competitors define the competitors in the game.

Buyers and Competitors in the Game

We can now return to how you would be sure to include Buyer 5 in a game analyzing the uptown apartment. Based on the initial assessment of which players to include in the game, you have four players: your firm (uptown), one competitor (harborside), and two buyers (Buyers 1 and 2). But if you look back at figure 12.1, you'll notice that once you've decided to include these four players, you need to include more. In particular, the competitor—harborside—has another buyer competing for it, namely Buyer 3. So you add Buyer 3 to the game. But because there is another firm competing for Buyer 3—the houseboat—you should include the houseboat. By continuing this reasoning, you can see that you will add Buyer 4, then the trailer, and, finally, Buyer 5.

The above reasoning shows that there is a sense in which you build a game. I make this procedure explicit below, again using the context of *Game 9.1* as an example. Before I do that, though, it is useful to establish the criteria for adding more players, given the players you already have. These criteria are essentially the same as the criteria stated above, except that I allow for the fact that you may have added more players than the initial buyers and competitors.

You should include a buyer in the game if, for some firm already in the game,

1. it knows about that firm (or can be made to know about it), *and*

2. it has a willingness to pay for that firm that exceeds the firm's marginal cost.

You should include a firm in the game if, for some buyer already in the game,

1. that buyer would consider doing business with the firm, *and*

2. the firm would react to a pricing decision by any of the existing firms in the game.

Let's return to *Game 9.1* to see how this works in practice. We start with the firm whose profitability we want to understand.

Step 0. Identify the firm we are interested in. This is the uptown firm.

Figure 12.0.0

Step 1. Identify buyers that meet our two criteria. These are Buyers 1 and 2.

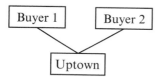

Figure 12.0.1

Step 2. Identify firms that meet our criteria. Buyer 1 is interested only in your apartment, but Buyer 2 would consider a harborside apartment. So, we include the harborside apartment.

Figure 12.0.2

Step 3. Identify buyers. We now have more firms in the game, so there might be additional buyers that meet our criteria. Buyers 2 and 3 meet the criteria for the harborside apartment. We already have Buyer 2, so we add Buyer 3. Our group of buyers now includes Buyers 1, 2, and 3.

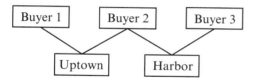

Figure 12.0.3

Step 4. Identify firms. Buyer 3 would consider a houseboat, so we add it to our set of competitors.

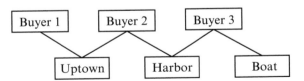

Figure 12.0.4

Step 5. Identify buyers. Buyers 3 and 4 meet the criteria for a houseboat. We already have Buyer 3, so we add Buyer 4. Our group of buyers now includes Buyers 1, 2, 3, and 4.

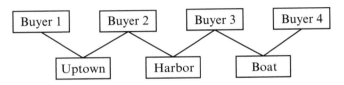

Figure 12.0.5

Step 6. Identify firms. Buyer 4 would consider a trailer home, so we add it to our set of competitors.

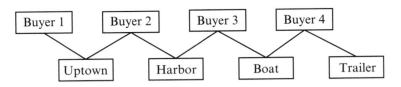

Figure 12.0.6

Step 7. Identify buyers. Buyers 4 and 5 meet the criteria for a trailer home. We already have Buyer 4, so we add Buyer 5. Our group of buyers now includes Buyers 1, 2, 3, 4, and 5.

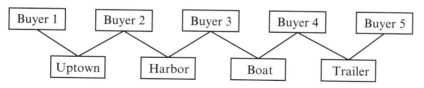

Figure 12.2
Completed player map

Step 8. Identify firms. Buyer 5 would consider only a trailer home, so our set of competitors is complete. Because we are not adding another firm, we know that our set of buyers is complete as well, so we are done. Figure 12.2 provides the player map for this game.

Although this example is complicated, it does emphasize the essential nature of deciding which players are relevant to you. In particular, it is not enough that you consider only your firm's buyers and competitors. Because of the possibility of market-price effects, you have to be prepared to consider competitors' buyers, competitors' competitors, and so on.

Players in the Game: The Broader Perspective

It is important not to lose sight of what this analysis tells you. You're trying to find out whether you can be profitable in a world of unrestricted competition. If you know that you have to be better, then it suffices to identify buyer segments in which you have a value-gap advantage. You need to worry only about your firm's competitors and, for each buyer segment, your value-gap advantage over the "best" competitor. You then have to assess whether you can capture some or all of those advantages. Finally, you need to assess whether the amount that you capture will cover your fixed costs.

If you cannot identify buyer segments in which you have a value-gap advantage, your only route to profitability—assuming unrestricted competition—is some form of excess supply. If you are fortunate enough to have excess demand for your products, then you can first check whether the price guaranteed you by an excluded or envious buyer provides enough profit to cover your fixed costs. If it doesn't, or if there is no excess demand for your products, then you'll need to consider all the relevant buyers and competitors, as in *Game 9.1*.

A Common Simplification

Because of linkages in buyer preferences, the process of identifying all the buyers and firms in a game can be complicated. In practice, most companies do not perform such a thorough analysis. Instead, they focus on just their buyers and competitors. How much do they miss by doing such a limited analysis? The answer, of course, depends on the specific context. Let's look at what this "shortcut" analysis would look like in *Game 9.1*. Figure 12.3 shows what this game would look like for the uptown apartment with this simplification. The apartment has no competitors, so we need only those buyers with a willingness to pay for the uptown apartment— Buyer 1 and Buyer 2.

From the figure, you can see that the key to using this simplified game is knowing enough to set Buyer 2's willingness to pay at $70. In other words, to use a simplified game, you need to adjust for any market-price effects that arise from players you are leaving out of the game. (If we had an example with excess supply, there would be a similar adjustment to some competitor's cost.) But if we need the complete game to determine these market-price effects, what is the point of this simplification? The answer is that in practice, firms often estimate these market-price effects

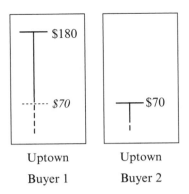

Figure 12.3
Game 9.1 simplified

empirically. By using past purchasing data and assumptions about buyer attributes, a firm might try to determine that the uptown apartment could command a price of at least $70. The main advantage of this empirical approach is that it can be much simpler. The main disadvantage—besides the usual issues around statistical estimation—is that it doesn't identify the reasons for the market-price effects. Consequently, the firm has less knowledge about what might cause the market price to shift dramatically. For instance, in *Game 9.1*, if the supply of trailer homes increased, the profits of all the firms would be dramatically reduced. This consequence can be deduced from the complete game in figure 12.1 but not from the simplified game in figure 12.3.

Market Size versus the Pie

When thinking about buyers, both current and potential, another common simplification is to consider the size of a market, rather than buyers and their willingnesses to pay. A firm usually computes (or estimates) this number by adding up all the current (or estimated) sales of all companies in its market. Although market size is a frequently cited number, it is one simplification that is less useful than you might imagine. Because profits are just a slice of a larger economic pie, the size of the pie is a far more useful number. Market-size calculations are based on only prices. As a result, they tell us almost nothing about how much value buyers and firms are capturing.

To be fair, comparing the different sizes of markets can give a sense of the relative size of the value creation in different markets, but this is a crude measure at best. For an example of how market size can be misleading, consider two different billion-dollar markets. In one, buyers are capturing very little value. In the other, buyers are capturing a lot of value—prices are way below buyers' willingnesses to pay. Suppose that in both markets, the prices of raw materials increase dramatically. Do firm profits suffer in both markets? No. In the first market, they certainly will suffer. Because buyers are capturing very little value, prices cannot rise without losing buyers. So either firm profits will drop or the market will shrink. But in the second market, it could easily be the case that firm profits are maintained and that buyer profits decrease. So, for both theoretical and practical reasons, we focus on the size of the pie, not the size of the "market."

Remember to Segment

In this chapter, I have focused on identifying the buyers and firms that are relevant to our firm's game. I'll end by noting that after identifying all of the buyers that should be in the game, there is still work to do. In order to assess your value-gap advantages, you have to remember to categorize the buyers into buyer segments. (In the examples in this chapter, each buyer corresponded to its own segment, so this task occurred naturally.)

13 Suppliers

To give you a basic understanding of profitability under unrestricted competition, I have focused on competition among buyers and firms. In many strategic situations, a firm's profitability depends crucially on interactions between competitors and buyers, so this is a natural starting point. But in my explanations so far, I've taken a firm's costs—which are also the prices the firm pays its suppliers—as given. I've treated suppliers as if they were outside the game. But there are situations in which suppliers, too, are actively involved in the creation and division of value, so let's look at how the presence of suppliers affects our analyses and when we should include them in the game.

Suppliers

In the games in parts II and III, there was a distinct difference between the way we treated a firm's costs and a firm's prices. A firm's prices were treated as a consequence of competition and bargaining, and we paid particularly close attention to the degree to which competition guaranteed prices. In contrast, we took a firm's costs as given. In theory, though, the prices a firm pays its suppliers—namely the firm's costs—are also a consequence of competition and bargaining. Thus, we should treat a firm's costs the same way we treated its prices. Figure 13.1 emphasizes this point.

In the figure, the total value created is no longer based on buyer willingnesses to pay and firm costs. Instead, it is based on buyer willingnesses to pay and *supplier* costs. The economic pie is then divided among three kinds of players. We still have buyer profit—namely willingness to pay minus price—and firm profit—price minus cost. But we are now including the supplier's economic profit: cost minus supplier's cost. (I use the term "cost" to denote a firm's cost—the price that a firm pays to a supplier. When we talk

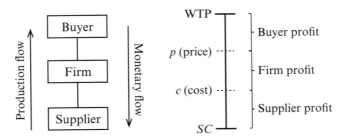

Figure 13.1
Value creation with suppliers

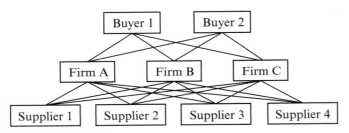

Figure 13.2
Game 13.1 player map

about a supplier's cost, we will always explicitly say "supplier" or use the abbreviation *SC*.) When we include suppliers in a game, the natural question is what costs will emerge under unrestricted competition. The method of analysis is the same, as the following example demonstrates.

In *Game 13.1*, we have one segment of two buyers, three firms, and four suppliers. To keep things as simple as possible, let's suppose that a supplier can provide a firm with everything required for production, including the labor to make the product. Furthermore, a supplier can supply only one firm at a cost of $20. In other words, each supplier has a supplier cost of $20 for supplying a firm. We will also suppose that each buyer wants only one unit from any of the three firms and has a willingness to pay of $50; see figures 13.2 and 13.3.

In this game, there is an excess of supply for the buyers and an excess of supply for the firms. Supply and demand intuition would suggest that all the profits will flow to the buyers, and this is indeed the case. Because there are only two buyers, the value creation will be based on the value created by two transactions:

TVC = 2(WTP − SC) = 2($50 − $20) = $60

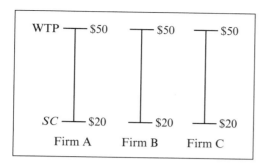

Figure 13.3
Game 13.1 value gaps

To see how this value will be divided, it suffices to consider the contributed values of each player. Only two suppliers are needed for value creation, so an individual supplier contributes zero. Similarly, only two firms are needed for value creation, so an individual firm contributes zero. Thus, the buyers must capture all the value.

To relate this outcome to figure 13.1, note that a supplier's profit will be $c - SC$. Because a supplier contributes zero, its profit must be zero, so we know that $c - SC = 0$. Due to competition, a firm will have to pay a supplier only $20. That's the good news. But a firm also contributes zero, so we know that $p - c = 0$. Due to competition, a buyer will have to pay only $20 for the product. That's the bad news for the firm. At a price of $20, each buyer captures $30, so, together, the buyers capture the whole pie.

This outcome should not surprise you. Both the suppliers and the firms are on the wrong side of the market, so they would have to be better to be profitable. But in this game, the suppliers were identical and the firms were identical, so neither could make a profit. To make things more interesting, we'll modify a firm and a supplier.

In *Game 13.2*, Firm A has a more efficient production process than the other two firms. As a result, a typical supplier's cost for serving Firm A is $15, as opposed to $20 for Firm B or C. Notice, by the way, that in the same way that a buyer can have a different willingness to pay for different firms, a supplier can have a different supplier's cost for different firms. This is demonstrated visually in the left panel of figure 13.4. Because Firm A is more efficient, the suppliers have a lower cost for supplying it.

The right panel of figure 13.4 shows that one of the suppliers—Supplier 1—is more efficient as well. Whereas the economic cost to supply Firm B or C is $20 for Suppliers 2, 3, and 4, it is only $17 for Supplier 1. Similarly, the economic cost to supply Firm A is $15 for Suppliers 2, 3, and 4, but only $12 for Supplier 1. As in *Game 13.1,* only the buyers are in a favorable supply and demand position, so we should expect them to

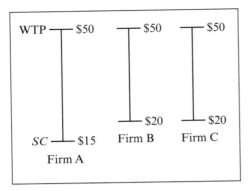

Supplier costs for Suppliers 2, 3, or 4

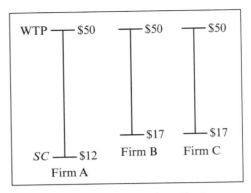

Supplier costs for Supplier 1

Figure 13.4
Game 13.2

capture most of the value creation. But both Firm A and Supplier 1 are better than their competition, so they also should be able to make a profit.

There are still only two buyers. Therefore, the value creation will be based again on the value created by two transactions. We know that Firm A and Supplier 1 must be involved in these two transactions, but we do not know whether Supplier 1 should supply Firm A or another firm. I have set up this example so that it does not matter, but, in general, it might. Therefore, it never hurts to explore the different possibilities. You merely try the different scenarios to see which yields the greatest value creation. For example:

Scenario 1   One buyer with Firm B (or C) and Supplier 1, the other buyer with Firm A and another supplier, yields ($50 – $17) + ($50 – $15) = $68.

Scenario 2   One buyer with Firm A and Supplier 1, the other buyer with Firm B (or C) and another supplier, yields ($50 – $12) + ($50 – $20) = $68.

In both scenarios, the total value created in $68, so either matching could occur under unrestricted competition.

Let's consider the contributed values. Firms B and C and Suppliers 2, 3, and 4 have zero contributed value, so they will capture nothing. Without Firm A, the value created would be

($50 – $17) + ($50 – $20) = $63

so Firm A contributes $5. Without Supplier 1, the value created would be

($50 – $15) + ($50 – $20) = $65

so Supplier 1 contributes $3. Without a buyer, Supplier 1 would transact with Firm A, and the value created would be

($50 − $12) = $38

so a buyer contributes $30. If we add up the contributed values of all the players, we see that they sum to the total pie: $30 + $30 + $5 + $3 = $68. So, in this example, competition completely determines the division of value.

Let's see what this value capture implies for the firms' costs and prices. Each buyer will capture $30, and each has a willingness to pay of $50, so the price p must equal $20. Firm A will capture $5, so its cost c must be $15. Firms B and C capture no value, so whichever firm transacts will have a cost c of $20. Finally, note that these costs imply that Supplier 1 receives a profit of $3. If Supplier 1 transacts with Firm B (or C), then $c—SC = $20 − $17 = 3. If Supplier 1 transacts with Firm A, then $c—SC = $15 − $12 = 3. I showed above that to maximize the value creation, it did not matter which firm Supplier 1 served. Consequently, the value capture should not depend on this either. In figure 13.5, I show how this is the case. In both scenarios, the price p is $20. In both scenarios, the cost c for Firm A is $15 and for Firm B (or C) is $20. Given these two facts, figure 13.5 shows that the value capture situation is the same in both scenarios.

Value Gaps with Suppliers

The addition of suppliers to a game does not affect the basic advice for profitability. If a firm has to compete for buyers, then it must identify buyer segments in which it has

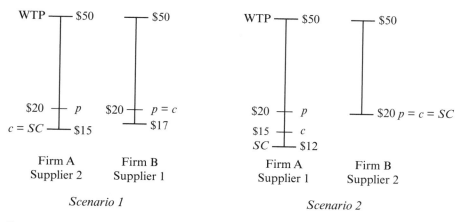

Figure 13.5
Game 13.2 analysis

a value-gap advantage. With suppliers, value gaps are computed with the suppliers' costs (SC) rather than with firms' costs (c). In *Game 13.1*, each firm has a value gap of $30, so no firm has an advantage. In games in which the suppliers differ in their supplier costs, the value-gap calculation can get complicated, but a good rule-of-thumb is to use supplier costs that are available to all of the relevant firms. In *Game 13.2*, for example, computing value gaps with Supplier 2, 3, or 4 provides the correct result: Firm A has a value-gap advantage over Firms B and C.

To see why using Supplier 1 in a value-gap calculation could be problematic, we consider a slightly more complicated game below. *Game 13.3* is the same as *Game 13.2*, except that Supplier 1 provides comparatively greater benefit to Firm B (or C) than to Firm A. If you analyze this game as we did above, you'll see that the pie is maximized when Supplier 1 transacts with Firm B or C, and Firm A transacts with one of the other suppliers, yielding value creation of $69 = ($50 − $16) + ($50 − $15). If you compute value-gap advantages using Supplier 1, it will appear that Firm A has only a value-gap advantage of $4 = ($50 − $12) − ($50 − $16). But this is incorrect. Firm A can capture up to $5—its contributed value. Because Supplier 1 can supply only one firm in this example, we do not know which firm, if any, will benefit from Supplier 1's advantage over the other suppliers. (In fact, Supplier 1 has a contributed value of $4 in this game, and it is guaranteed $3 of this $4. The split of the remaining dollar is due to bargaining between Supplier 1 and the *buyers*. Figure 13.7 depicts the outcomes for this game.) Consequently, for a conservative assessment of value gaps, we use supplier costs that are available to all of the relevant firms.

Profit Flow

Games 13.2 and *13.3* are structured in such a way that almost all of the profits will end up with the buyers, except for some profits that firms with an advantage and suppliers with an advantage will capture. This represents the pessimistic base case of the strategy field: you will always have to compete for buyers. But it is useful to remember that the supply and demand balances can cause the bulk of profits to flow to both suppliers and firms, as well. Figure 13.8 presents four stylized player maps to emphasize this point.

The first diagram corresponds to situations like those in *Games 13.1*, *13.2*, and *13.3*. There is more firm capacity than there are buyers and more supplier capacity than firm capacity. Only the buyers are in a favorable supply–demand scenario, so the bulk of the profits will flow to them. In the second diagram, profits will flow to the suppliers. You can think of the suppliers as a small group controlling a scarce resource. There will be

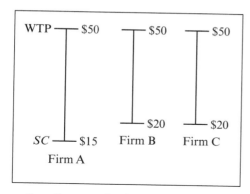

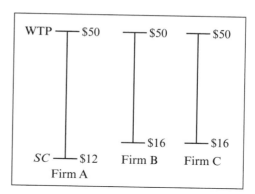

Supplier costs for Suppliers 2, 3, or 4

Supplier costs for Supplier 1

Figure 13.6
Game 13.3

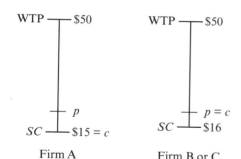

Both buyers will pay the same price, *p*, between $19 and $20.

Firm A

Supplier 2, 3, or 4

Firm B or C

Supplier 1

Figure 13.7
Game 13.3 analysis

Figure 13.8
Generic supply–demand balances and profit flows

an excess of firms that want this resource, and if the firms that transact with the suppliers face an even greater buyer demand, the suppliers will capture most of the pie. The third diagram depicts what must be true for the firms to capture most of the pie: excess buyer demand and excess supplier supply.

The fourth diagram corresponds to a more complicated story. There is an excess of firm supply, so firms will only be able to capture value-gap advantages. The bulk of the value capture will flow to either the buyers or the suppliers. But which? We can't be sure. If buyer demand is roughly equivalent to supplier capacity, it could go either way. What we're sure about is that it will be very painful for the firms, which will be squeezed by both buyers and suppliers. Competition for buyers will lead firms to have lower prices, and competition for suppliers will lead firms to pay their suppliers more—that is, to have higher costs. Even for those firms with value-gap advantages, this is a treacherous context for trying to be profitable.

Suppliers in the Game

Having considered how the presence of suppliers can affect a business game, you now need to ask: Which suppliers, if any, should be included in the game? There are two criteria for including a supplier in your game. The first is analogous to the two criteria for a relevant buyer:

1. The supplier must be aware of your firm as a potential buyer and be willing to transact with your firm.

This might seem obvious, and the first part of it certainly is. In contrast with a buyer, it is easy to make a supplier aware that you might want to transact with it—you just let the supplier know that you are interested in acquiring its product or service. But the second part is not so obvious, as there are cases in which a supplier might not be interested in transacting with a firm. For instance, employees are an important type of supplier, and there certainly are jobs that a person might turn down at any practical price.

The second criterion is similar to one of the criteria for a competitor:

2. The price paid to the supplier (your firm's cost) depends on unrestricted competition among the other players in the game.

This second criterion addresses a practical issue with a firm's costs. A firm will treat some of its costs as given (e.g., a small firm's electricity bill). There will be a price for the supply, and the firm can choose whether or not to purchase the supply. In such cases, the price that the firm pays to the supplier will not be subject to the force of competition, so we leave such a supplier out of the game.

In other cases, though, the price paid to the supplier will be subject to the force of competition, so you'll want to include that supplier in the game. Because you need to distinguish between these two types of suppliers—those that might affect your analysis and those whose prices (to your firm) you can take as fixed—we have our second criterion.

Accounting for Suppliers Both In and Out of the Game

The decision to leave a supplier out of your analysis is always a practical one. If we view the firm's payments to the supplier as given, it simplifies matters to leave the supplier out of the game. But this increase in simplicity is not free. When some of a firm's costs are given and some are treated as the consequence of unrestricted competition with suppliers, we have to be careful when we translate value capture into prices and costs. I'll use a simple example to demonstrate the issue.

In *Game 13.4*, we have one buyer, one firm, and one supplier. The supplier is an employee with an economic cost of $80 thousand to work for the firm. Additionally, the firm will incur costs of $50 thousand to cover materials, rent, and so on. The firm has no control over the cost of these supplies, so we treat their providers as outside the game. The buyer has a willingness to pay of $200 thousand for the firm's product. In this game, there is value creation of $70 thousand, and each player has a contributed value of $70 thousand, so value capture will be due solely to bargaining among the supplier, the firm, and the buyer. Let's suppose, for instance, that the players negotiate a $20, $20, $30 split among supplier, firm, and buyer, respectively. This would imply that the buyer pays a price of $170 thousand and the firm pays the supplier $100 thousand. But $100 thousand is not the firm's cost—we have to remember to add in the additional $50 thousand to get the total firm cost, c. Figure 13.9 is designed to emphasize this fact. In the figure, the subscript S is used to identify the portion of supplier costs (SC) and firm cost (c) attributable to the transaction with the supplier.

As figure 13.9 shows, when your business game includes some, but not all, of your firm's suppliers, firm costs will be based on both costs that are the consequence of competition with suppliers—c_s in figure 13.9—and costs that can be taken as fixed—the $50 in figure 13.9.

Competitors Revisited

If the prices paid to suppliers are a consequence of competition, who is involved in this competition? As a firm, you would hope that suppliers are competing to serve you. But

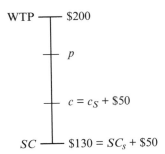

Figure 13.9
Game 13.4

it might also be the case that you have to compete for a supplier. If so, who would your competitors be? Would they be the same firms with whom you compete for buyers? Not necessarily. For example, both investment banks and consulting firms compete for graduates from the world's top business schools, but they do not generally compete for the same buyers. So, by including suppliers in a game, you might also need to account for another type of competitor. We call such competitors *supplier-side* competitors. (We could use the terms "buyer-side competitors" and 'both-side competitors' to describe, respectively, players with whom we compete for buyers and players with whom we compete for both buyers and suppliers. But because the term "competitor" is usually interpreted to mean a buyer-side or both-side competitor, this precision is typically more cumbersome than useful.) In many cases, the players competing for your suppliers will be the same as the players competing for your buyers. If so, you won't have to include any additional competitors when adding suppliers into your game. But as our example showed, they might not be the same competitors, so you need to be prepared to think about additional competitors with respect to your suppliers.

The definition of a supplier-side competitor mirrors the definition of a buyer-side competitor. A supplier-side competitor is a relevant player if

1. a relevant supplier would consider doing business with it, *and*
2. it will react to your bargaining with the supplier (i.e., they see you as a competitor for the supplier).

Suppliers and Competitors in the Game

In the discussion of buyers and competitors, I noted that identifying buyers and competitors required, in general, an iterative process. Starting with your firm, you identified your buyers, then your competitors, then additional buyers that could be interested in your competitors, then additional firms that could serve the additional buyers, and so on. In theory, you would undertake the same process with suppliers. Having identified your suppliers, you would identify any supplier-side competitors, then any additional suppliers for these competitors, then any additional competitors for these additional suppliers, and so on.

In practice, though, it usually suffices to consider only your firm's suppliers and competitors for those suppliers. This is similar to the simplification I described for buyers and competitors, and the issues are the same. In particular, you need to understand how market-price effects could affect your suppliers' economic costs for serving your firm and your supplier-side competitors. In contrast to buyers, a firm's suppliers' costs often are based on easily understood market prices. And for those inputs that are not based on standard market prices, the firms in the industry often know the firms that need the inputs—and the reason that they need them. Thus, understanding your competitors' preferences for suppliers is typically a far simpler task than understanding buyers' preferences. Consequently, firms are in a better position to understand the market-price effects on supplier costs without including all the supplier-side competitors, additional suppliers for these competitors, additional competitors for these additional suppliers, and so on.

14 Larger Games

Since a firm's profits are ultimately determined by its revenues and costs, it is natural to focus on your firm's interactions with buyers, competitors, and suppliers. In most cases, looking at these three categories of players will give you an understanding of a firm's profitability. For some companies, though, looking at a larger game will provide a better understanding of their profitability. In this chapter, we look at two specific examples of larger games—games with more stages and games with complements.

Multiple Stages

Another look at figure 13.1 will remind you that a firm's profits are bounded by the willingnesses to pay of its buyers and the costs of its suppliers. But sometimes the willingness to pay we really care about is not our buyer's willingness to pay, but the willingness to pay of, say, our buyer's buyer. In such cases, you will want to include more than the three stages of suppliers, firms, and buyers. For instance, consider the maker of a branded soft-drink syrup, such as Coca-Cola. Its buyers are bottlers. Bottlers sell to distributors. Distributers sell to supermarkets. Supermarkets sell to consumers. If we were to analyze Coca-Cola, we would want to identify buyer segments in which Coke had a value-gap advantage over Pepsi and store brands. But we wouldn't want to use bottlers' willingnesses to pay in computing value gaps. We would want consumers' willingnesses to pay. Consequently, we would want our game to include multiple stages, as shown in figure 14.1. (In this figure, *SC* denotes the syrup maker's economic cost.)

Though less frequent, a similar situation can occur on the supplier side. If your company has a cost advantage because it uses, say, a rare earth mineral that is cheaper than the mineral that your competitors use, then you want your game to reflect that

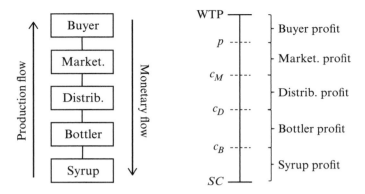

Figure 14.1
Value creation: multiple stages from firm to buyer

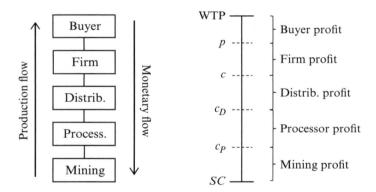

Figure 14.2
Value creation: multiple stages from firm to supplier

fact, as shown in the right-hand value gap in figure 14.2. In the figure, we assume that the mining company sells to a processing company, which, in turn, sells to a distributor.

One nice feature about figures 14.1 and 14.2 is that they show the stages at which players try to make a profit. In other words, they show how many ways the players will try to "slice" the economic pie. When looking at such a picture, a fundamental question is whether so many stages are necessary. Often the players in the middle are called intermediaries, and the process of trying to eliminate them is disintermediation. Currently, many businesses are being threatened by disintermediation, and participants in those businesses are complaining about being driven out of business. Consider travel agents. With the growth of the web and Internet access, many people do not use travel agents as much, and many travel agencies are hurting. From a strategy perspective, the central question is whether or not disintermediation increases the pie. If travel agencies were an inefficient way to match buyers to travel services, then disintermediation would be inevitable. But if travel agencies provided a personalized service that could not be replicated by access to the web, then some agencies should be able to survive profitably.

Thus, if your firm is in a business in which the buyers' willingnesses to pay are several stages removed from you, including the stages in your analysis would provide two benefits: the essential willingness to pay is included in your value gap, and you are reminded to assess the need for the intermediaries.

Firm Complements

In all the games considered so far, we have discussed a buyer's willingness to pay for different products, but we have not talked about a buyer's willingness to pay for a collection of products. In general, this does not cause a problem if the other products are readily available. For instance, your willingness to pay for a computer would drop significantly if software were not available. But when we talk about willingness to pay for different computers, we are implicitly assuming that software is available at relatively fixed prices. In other words, we are treating the software companies as players outside of the game. Hardware and software are an example of what we call firm *complements*, and I discuss them in this section. In the next section, I'll discuss complementarity more generally.

There are two kinds of firm complements—those that enhance a buyer's willingness to pay for a firm and those that reduce a supplier's cost of serving a firm. On the buyer side, two firms are complements if the willingness to pay for the products together is greater than the sum of the individual willingnesses to pay. In the case of a computer and software, this would mean that

WTP(computer and software) > WTP (computer alone) + WTP (software alone)

This joint gain in willingness to pay is the key attribute that identifies firms as complements. But we also need to assess whether a complementary firm should be included in our analysis—that is, whether it is a relevant player. This leads to the following criteria.

Firm B should be included in Firm A's game (as a buyer-side complement) if

1. there is a joint gain in willingness to pay, namely WTP(Firm A and Firm B) > WTP(Firm A) + WTP(Firm B); and

2. Firm B might react to Firm A's pricing decisions.

Again, it is important to emphasize that in the analysis of many situations, we leave the complementary player out of the game. The reason is implied by the second criterion—we don't believe that the complementary firm will change its prices based on what our firm will do. Thus, for example, when analyzing a car company, we would typically leave out the gas companies, because we don't believe that the price of gas will react to the price of automobiles.

For a firm to be a complement with respect to a supplier, consider two firms that each need 50 units of a particular part from a supplier. Suppose that to make these parts, the supplier has to incur a fixed setup cost of $100 and a per-unit cost of $2. Its cost to serve either firm alone is $200, but it can serve both firms for $300:

SC(Firm A and Firm B) = $300 < SC(Firm A) + SC(Firm B) = $200 + $200

In this example, Firm A and Firm B are complements because the supplier can serve them both for a lower total cost than if it served them individually. So we have these additional criteria:

Firm B should be included in Firm A's game (as a supplier-side complement) if

1. there is a joint savings in supplier cost, namely SC(Firm A and Firm B) < SC(Firm A) + SC(Firm B); and

2. Firm B will react to Firm A's pricing decisions.

One curious fact to note is that a firm can be both a competitor and a complement. This often happens when firms are complements with respect to a supplier. The previous example is fairly common. If two competitors use the same supplier, and if the supplier has significant economies of scale in producing its products, then there is a good chance that the competitors are also complements.

Having identified relevant complements, how do they affect your firm's profits? To answer this question, I'll use an example that starts with the complementary firm being out of the game.

Consider a buyer that is interested in buying one of two computers, provided that he can also buy a special software application. (Without this software, the buyer has no willingness to pay for a computer.) The buyer has a willingness to pay of $1,400 for a Firm A computer with software and $1,200 for a Firm B computer with software. (Suppose, say, that Firm A's computer has a higher resolution display.) Suppose that the costs for Firms A and B are $600 and $500, respectively, and that the cost for the software company is $300. If the buyer is sure that he can purchase the software for $400, then we can leave the software firm out of the game. The left-hand panel of figure 14.3 depicts the game. Note that the buyers' willingnesses to pay have been reduced by $400 to account for their payment to the software company.

The game without the complement is like our previous examples, and Firm A should win the buyer because of its larger value gap. But now suppose that the buyer believes that there is not a fixed price for the software. We would then have the game in the right-hand panel of figure 14.3. Firm A should still win the buyer, but the division of value will be more complicated. With the complement not in the game, the buyer and Firm A would bargain over Firm A's value-gap advantage—namely $100. (The software company was assumed to capture a profit of $100.) When the complement is added into the game, Firm A still has to bargain for its value-gap advantage, but the bargaining now includes the complement, as well. Because the contributed value of the software company is the whole pie, the software company is in the same position as the buyer when it comes to dividing the value creation. Thus, Firm A now has to contend with the complement, as well as with the buyer, in trying to capture its advantage.

This example demonstrates two points regarding the impact of firm complements on profitability. First, firm complements are far more prevalent than you might imagine, but their effect is seen implicitly in willingness-to-pay calculations (or supplier cost calculations for complements on the supplier side.) Because the price of

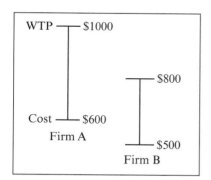

(Assumed) software profit = $100
Buyer profit: $300 to $400
Firm A profit: 0 to $100

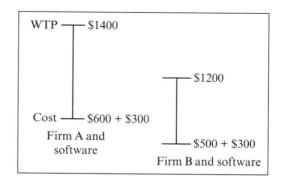

Software profit: 0 to $500
Buyer profit: 0 to $500
Firm A profit: 0 to $100

Figure 14.3
Game without and with a firm complement

the complement is often taken as fixed—as in the example, mentioned above, of the price of gas not reacting to the price of automobiles—when analyzing a company of interest, it is left out of the game, so it does not affect our analysis of a firm's profitability.

Second, when a unique complement should be included in the game, the division of the pie will typically depend more on bargaining and less on competition. For instance, in the right-hand game in figure 14.3, both hardware and software are needed for value creation. Because there is no value creation without the software company, competition has nothing to say about the division of value between the buyer and the software company.

If the complement is not unique, though, competition does affect the division of value in a predictable way. In the game in figure 14.3, if two competing firms were offering software, if the buyer viewed them as equally good, and if they had the same costs, then the complements would capture nothing. The buyer would be guaranteed a profit of $400, and the buyer and Firm A would bargain over the remaining $100 of value. If one competing complement were better than another, then the "better" complement would have potential profit. A firm complement is better than another if it increases the value gap by a larger amount. Figure 14.4 provides an example.

In this example, I have labeled the original software company "Software A" and added a second software company, "Software B." For simplicity, I have assumed that both software companies have the same costs: $300. Notice that I have provided four

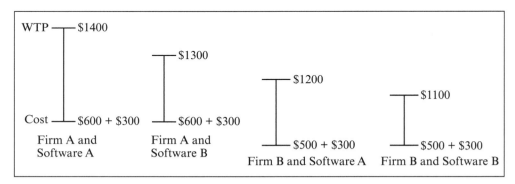

Software A profit: 0 to $100
Buyer profit: $300 to $500
Firm A profit: 0 to $100

Figure 14.4
Competing complements

value gaps—one for each combination of firm and complement. With these four value gaps, it is easy to identify each player's contributed value. In particular, note that Software A has a contributed value of $100. (The buyer, Firm A, and Software B can create $400 of value without Software A.) This is the answer we would expect. Although competition is limiting Software A's value capture, it has a potential profit of $100—the amount by which it is better than the competition in terms of value creation.

Complementarity

As the preceding examples suggest, understanding value creation often requires an understanding of complementarity, even if the complements are not active players in the game. You're not going to have much success selling automobiles in a part of the world with few roads. And if your product relies on a part that can be feasibly produced only in volumes greater than you need, you're going to need other firms that also need the part. But complementarity is more general—and thus more important—than just firm complementarity. If competition leads to a stable outcome, then complementarity, in some form, is present in all value creation. In other words, if there is value creation, there is complementarity. To demonstrate this fact, we'll start with a general definition of complements and then consider some examples.

Two players, A and B, are complements if the sum of their contributed values equals or exceeds their combined contributed value:

$$\text{ConV(Player A)} + \text{ConV(Player B)} \geq \text{ConV(Player A \& Player B)}$$

For an example of this equation, recall the right-hand game of figure 14.3. In that game, the contributed values of Firm A and the software company were $100 and $500, respectively. Thus,

$$\text{ConV(Firm A)} + \text{ConV(Software)} = \$600 > \text{ConV(Firm A \& Software)} = \$500$$

For another example, consider a case of complementarity that is often overlooked: a simple deal between a buyer and a seller. As we saw back in our first game—*Game 2.1*—the contributed value of each player is the whole pie. Thus, we clearly have

$$\text{ConV(Buyer)} + \text{ConV(Seller)} = 2 \text{ Pies} > \text{ConV(Buyer \& Seller)} = \text{Pie}$$

This example is important because it emphasizes that the simplest of deals is an exercise in complementary value creation. For contrast, consider how negotiators often describe such a deal as a "zero-sum" negotiation over price. But it is obviously not zero-sum. If a price is agreed upon, there will be value creation, as our formal definition of complementarity implies.

Complementarity can also be defined for groups of players. Two groups of players, say A and B, are complements if the sum of their contributed values exceeds their combined contributed value:

ConV(Goup A) + ConV(Group B) > ConV(Group A & Group B)

For a simple example of group complementarity, think of a game with just buyers and firms. In such a case, the group of all the buyers and the group of all the firms are complements. Without any buyers, no value is created, so the contributed value of the buyers as a group is the whole pie. Similarly, the contributed value of the firms as a group is the whole pie. So we have a situation similar to the simple buyer–seller game:

ConV(Buyers) + ConV(Firms) = 2 Pies > ConV(Buyers & Firms) = Pie

True, this is not a very interesting example, particularly because one of the sides will usually capture much less than the pie. But thinking in terms of group complementarity is useful in other situations.

For instance, consider the providers of marketplaces, whether it is someone providing a backyard for a garage sale, a field for a flea market, or an online trading platform. In all these cases, the marketplace provider is a complement.

Or consider a professional sports team. In one sense, the players are sellers and the audience is buyers. Yet there is a group called "owners" that profits, as well. Should we think of the owners as firms and the players as suppliers? We can, but the important point is that all three groups—players, owners, and audience—are complementary from a value-creation perspective.

Finally, we saw above how competitors could be firm complements, especially with respect to a supplier. For similar reasons, buyers and suppliers also can be complements. (Remember, a firm is just a buyer with respect to a supplier and a supplier with respect to a buyer.) In fact, suppliers are often complements. If you need butter and sugar to make a cookie, then butter and sugar—the "suppliers" for your cookie—are complements. Similarly, any two suppliers that provide critical parts for a firm's products are complementary. And you and your coworkers are typically complements, as well.

In short, complementarity is pervasive in value creation. As I noted above, if there is value creation, there is complementarity. The practical implication of this fact follows from the following logic: To understand your profits, you have to understand the pie from which they are taken. And to understand the pie, you have to understand that value creation is a complementary activity, even in the simple case of a buyer–seller transaction.

15   Economic Value: Relative and Subjective

In the last three chapters, we focused on one of the most important judgments for understanding firm profitability: which players should be in the game or, in other words, who matters. In many cases, this judgment implies a judgment about the size of the pie. If you look back at figure 14.3, for instance, you'll see that the total value created is either $500 or $400, depending on whether or not you include the software company in the game. This suggests that value creation is relative rather than fixed. If you believe that value creation should be some sort of absolute measure, this might seem disconcerting. In this chapter, you'll see that it is actually quite natural for value creation to be a relative concept.

Value Creation Is Relative

Let's consider an intuitive example. Suppose that you are interested in buying a TV set. You spend the day looking at TVs in several large electronics stores and finally decide which model you want. As it happens, all of the stores are charging the same price for this particular model: $400. On your way home, you decide to stop in just one more store, and you find that this store also has the model you want, and with the same $400 price tag. There is a difference, though: this is a small store, and the owner is there. So you decide to try negotiating a price lower than the listed price. You are somewhat persuasive, and after a little back and forth, you agree to buy the TV for $350. You go home happy, feeling as if you have just made $50.

What value has been created in this deal? Let's suppose that the store's cost for the TV is $325. Thus, the value creation is $75, and so you have captured two-thirds of the pie. But then you remember reading a story in *TV Guide*. A while back, a polling firm had asked TV viewers how much money they would accept to give up watching TV. It was reported that almost half of the viewers would need to be paid at least $1,000,000 to give up watching TV. Now, you may not be that fanatical about TV—after all, a million dollars is a lot of money—but if you had to, you would probably pay thousands of dollars, if not tens of thousands of dollars, for the ability to watch TV. So, for the mere cost of $350, it seems as if you have received thousands of dollars of benefit. In other words, it seems as if the pie is a lot larger than $75, and you made a lot more than $50 when you bought your new TV.

So, just how well did you do when you bought your new TV for $350? Did you capture $50 of value, or did you capture thousands of dollars of value? The answer is actually "yes." Both answers are correct, though strictly speaking, the answers are incomplete. You captured $50 in the game with just you and the seller. You captured thousands of dollars in a game with all the providers of TV and all the buyers of TVs. That is, we can talk about value creation and value capture only relative to some context or, put differently, relative to some game. Whether you captured $50 of value or thousands of dollars of value is a matter of perspective—the perspective of how many players you include in the game.

I should emphasize that just because value is relative, it is not arbitrary. To understand why, let's consider another situation in which a relative measurement is anything but arbitrary. Suppose that we want to describe where New York City is. We could say that it is about 200 miles south of Boston. Or we could say that it is about 3,000 miles east of San Francisco. Both of these are relevant statements. But there is nothing arbitrary about the physical location of New York City. In a similar way, when we define economic value, it is relative, but it is certainly not arbitrary.

To describe the location of New York City, we used another city as a reference point. To define economic value, the relevant "reference point" is the collection of people involved. So, economic value must be defined relative to a group of people. Consider our TV example again. If the group of people consists of just you and the TV store owner, then you have, in fact, captured $50 of value. Your best option outside of this group was a price of $400. So with respect to this outside option, you are $50 better off: $400 minus $350. But now consider the group containing every person that could be involved in providing you with TV service. This would include every TV manufacturer, all the networks, all the cable operators, and so on. Your best option outside of this group is no TV in your life at all. As we noted above, you might pay thousands of dollars to avoid a life without TV. So, relative to this much larger group, you have captured thousands of dollars of value (because thousands of dollars minus $350 still equals thousands of dollars). In both cases, the value you captured is far from an arbitrary amount. But it is relevant to the group of people you want to consider.

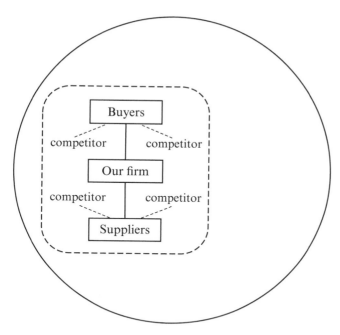

Figure 15.1
Value creation within a larger economic world

At this point, I'm hoping that you remembered why we were so careful about defining a buyer's willingness to pay and a seller's economic cost based on options "outside of the game." Because value creation is relative, we needed a fixed reference point. In fact, the total value created in a game is always part of a larger game. Figure 15.1 emphasizes this point.

In the rounded, dashed rectangle we have a game with buyers, competitors (both on the buyer and supplier side), suppliers, and our firm. The total value created in this game is nothing more than the economic value that this group of players collectively contributes to the larger economic environment; see figure 15.2.

The question of which players to include in a game and which to leave out is sometimes called the boundary of the game question. In the figures above, you can see why. The rounded, dashed rectangle is the boundary. In a game with just a few players, the boundary will be small. With a large number of players, it will be large.

The previous chapters provided guidelines about where to draw the boundary. You should always include players who would be actively involved in the competition and bargaining for prices, but you can exclude players who would not be involved. In our

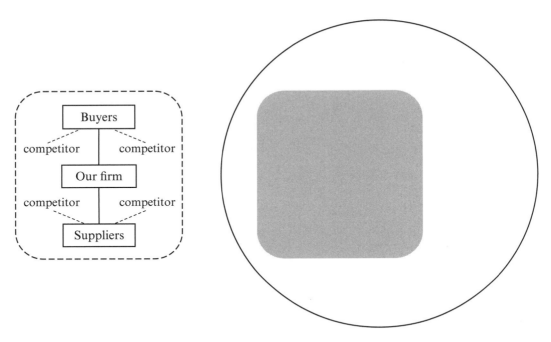

Figure 15.2
TVC of a game as contribution to the larger economic world

TV example, we most likely would have modeled the game with just the buyer and seller, for a total value creation of $75. But it is sometimes useful to consider a much larger game. For instance, in a consumer society like that of the United States, people often complain about the prices they pay for goods. But take one of your favorite products, and imagine the much larger game in which the outside option is a world without that product. You might find that your willingness to pay in this much larger game is quite large—much like a $1,000,000 willingness to pay for TV. From the perspective of the larger game, you might find that you are appropriating a huge amount of value.

Value Creation Is Subjective

Figures 15.1 and 15.2 are designed to emphasize the fact that value is relative. But they also can show us that value can be subjective. In figure 15.3, I've added a reminder about how buyers' willingnesses to pay and suppliers' costs are calculated—they are based on options outside the game. Note, though, that an option *outside* of a game is *inside* the larger economic context.

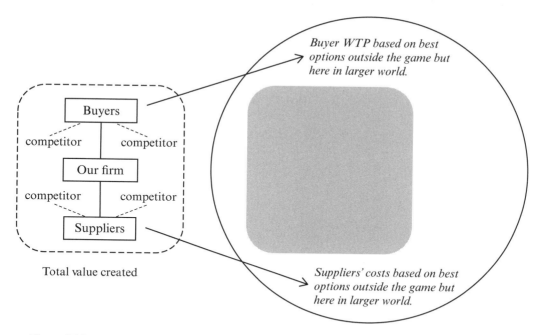

Buyer WTP based on best options outside the game but here in larger world.

Suppliers' costs based on best options outside the game but here in larger world.

Buyers

competitor   competitor

Our firm

competitor   competitor

Suppliers

Total value created

Figure 15.3

Outside options are inside the larger economic world

If you recall our discussion of willingness to pay and economic cost, you'll remember that outside options can be objective or subjective. For instance, a buyer's willingness to pay for an industrial product might be based on an alternative solution, whereas its willingness to pay for a consumer product could be based solely on the buyer's desire for the product. In the case in which both buyer willingnesses to pay and supplier costs are subjective, we have the curious case in which a firm's profits—which are very definitely objective—are part of subjectively determined value creation. We have a subjective slice of an objective pie (see figure 15.4).

In our TV example, the buyer's profit of $50 in the two-player game was objective. The buyer's willingness to pay was based on an outside alternative priced at $400. But in the much larger game, the buyer's value capture was subjective. Can the same thing happen with a firm's profit? If we consider a much larger game, will the firm's range of possible profits increase and become subjective? Possibly, but not necessarily. There are many situations in which a firm's range of profits remains the same as the game is enlarged. In particular, if a firm's profits are based on its value-gap advantages, then considering a larger boundary for the game will usually not change its profits. Because

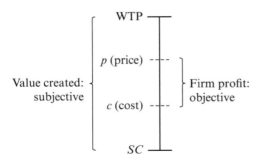

Figure 15.4
An objective slice of a subjective pie

the firm's profits are based on value-gap advantages, profits are determined by a "next-best" competitor. As long as the increase in the size of the game does not generate excess demand, the presence of the next-best competitor will still be the main determinant of the firm's profits. Thus, the firm's profits will not change, though the total value created most likely will increase.

When the Boundary of the Game Doesn't Matter

We have seen how the boundary of the game affects both value creation and value capture. It will always affect value creation because value creation is a relative measure that depends on the players that we include in the game. And in some cases it also can affect a firm's value capture. But are there conditions under which we don't have to be careful of where we draw the boundary? In other words, are there conditions under which each player's value capture is not affected by the players that are included in the game? In general, the answer is "no." The reason is that competition and bargaining determine profits. When we decide to include some players and omit others, we usually have to make some assumption about what happened in the bargaining with the omitted players. We can see this in the game from figure 14.3, which is shown again in figure 15.5.

If the software company is omitted from the game, then we have to make an assumption about what price it would have received from the buyer. (We assumed a price of $400 in this example.) By contrast, if the software company is included, no such assumption needs to be made. As a consequence, there is a larger range of possible outcomes for both the buyer and the software company.

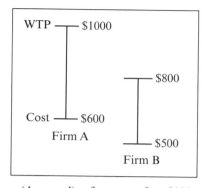
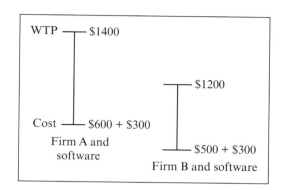

(Assumed) software profit = $100
Buyer profit: $300 to $400
Firm A profit: 0 to $100

Software profit: 0 to $500
Buyer profit: 0 to $500
Firm A profit: 0 to $100

Figure 15.5
Omitted complementor assumed to receive price of $400

Therefore, the judgment about the boundary of the game is critical because it often requires an assumption about bargaining. But what if prices in a game are determined solely by competition, not by both competition and bargaining? Would the boundary of the game still affect player profits? The answer is "no." This is the one situation in which the boundary of the game does not "matter." Formally, this is a game in which every player receives its contributed value. Because we know that a player cannot get more than its contributed value when competition is unrestricted, we have the following two facts:

Fact 1. Each player in a game can receive its contributed value if, and only if, adding up each player's contributed value equals the total value created.

Fact 2. Consider a game in which adding up each player's contributed value equals the total value created. Take some players out of the game. In the remaining smaller game, adding up each player's contributed value equals the total value created.

This "adding-up" scenario is a special case, and some economists use "perfect competition" —shorthand for "competition perfectly determines prices" —to describe it. This is equivalent to saying that "competition eliminates any bargaining." But because perfect competition does not happen that often, the practical advice is to know that when constructing a game, there is a good chance that your assessment of players' outside options depends on an assumption about bargaining (as in figure 15.5). Thus, you should be aware of this assumption.

V Changes in the Game

16   Sustaining Profitability

In the first four parts of this book, I described how to think about the profitability of your business. By viewing your situation as a business game, you can ask and answer the simple question of whether your firm can be profitable. But what would you do if your situation changed? Then you would need a new game to describe your different circumstances, and you would analyze that new game. In this part of the book, we'll look at some of the ways in which the game can change. Ideally, we would like to *predict* how the game can change and whether the changes would be beneficial or detrimental to our firm's profitability. Since we can't predict the future, this is obviously not going to be a comprehensive guide to predicting future profitability. But there are some insights we can extract from the theory, and I present them here. In this chapter, we'll consider a classic strategy question. Assuming that we are profitable today, will we continue to be profitable in the future? In the strategy field this is sometimes called the sustainability question, as in "is our current profitability sustainable?"

From the perspective of value creation and capture, the question of sustainable profits splits into two parts:

1. Is the pie—the total value created—going to change?

2. Is our share of the pie going to change?

The reasons for these two questions are almost self-evident. If no value is created, then no value can be captured. Thus, to begin, we must ask whether the pie will persist. Assuming that the answer is affirmative—the total value created will not disappear—we come to the second question: Will we continue to capture value—that is, will we continue to make money? In short, because a firm's profit is a piece of a larger pie, there are two ways that this piece can shrink: the pie itself can shrink—the firm has a smaller piece of a smaller pie—or other players can take some of the piece—the firm ends up with a smaller piece of the same pie.

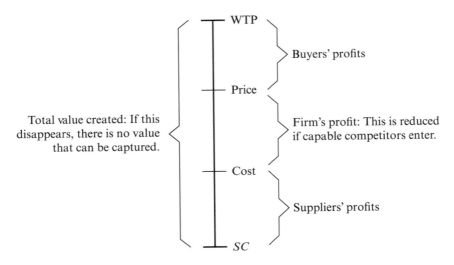

Figure 16.1
Sustainability of the pie and share of pie

Figure 16.1 depicts the two possibilities. The business strategy field has traditionally been more focused on the second issue: a firm's profits decreasing due to competition. Consequently, it is often argued that sustainable profits need a way to keep competition out, and the term "barrier to entry" is used to describe such ways. This is part of the story, but you also need to make sure that there is some value creation to bar the competitors from entering, as it were. So in this chapter, we will also look at whether the value created is likely to survive over time.

Assessing the Sustainability of the Pie

As figure 16.1 reminds us, to sustain the total value created over time, we want buyer WTP to neither decrease nor disappear altogether, and we want suppliers' costs not to increase much, if at all. (We include suppliers here rather than just considering firm costs because, in practice, supplier costs are often a source of a shrinking pie. For instance, think of increases in labor costs or oil prices.)

Will buyer WTP for your products and your competitors' products persist? Answering this question requires you to predict customer behavior. Arguably, this is the most difficult task in business. Understanding current customer behavior is difficult enough, but predicting future behavior is as difficult a job as you'll find in business. You need to assess the sustainability of your buyers' WTP, but there is no universally accepted mechanism for doing that. However, macroeconomists and security analysts do try to forecast buyer WTP at an aggregate level—for instance, how the market for consumer durables will change. And while that approach to forecasting is often broader than you'll want—that is, you are concerned with the WTP for *your* products, not the demand for a broad category of products—it's still better than nothing.

Predicting what will happen with suppliers' costs is only slightly less difficult. To do so, you have to assess the labor markets for your employees, the trend in prices for any commodities you use, and the alternative demand for any specialized supplies you use. Even harder, you have to predict whether dramatic improvements will occur in the technologies you use and whether new technologies will emerge. Predicting technological innovation is, in fact, virtually impossible, but the good news is that such innovations tend to increase the pie, not reduce it. The bad news is that your competitors might acquire that superior technology before you do. And while this would increase the pie, it could decrease your firm's profit.

Looking at this question from a slightly different perspective, asking whether the pie will survive is like asking whether the game itself will survive. Interestingly, there hasn't been much written in the business strategy literature about *game* survival. A lot has been written about the survival of products and services—the history of business is filled with examples of products and services that were once in great demand but for which there is no longer a market. For instance, think of how the introduction of zippers shrank the market for buttons or how the introduction of Velcro shrank the market for zippers and laces. In both of these cases, it would appear that the game shrank dramatically because buyer WTP for the product shrank dramatically.

Later in this chapter, though, you'll see that all is not necessarily lost if buyers' WTP disappears for our *products and services*. The key insight here is the need to consider the viability of the 'underlying' product or service. In other words, if you're in the business of producing laces for shoes, the game is over, and you're out of business. But, if you're in the shoe *fastener* business, then value is still being created in the game, and if you can adapt, you might be able to contribute value, as well. Thus the question of the pie being sustained—of the game surviving—is far subtler than the question of preference for a particular product surviving.

Finally, it's important to remember that value creation, if it is changing, doesn't always change in one irreversible direction—that is, either steadily increasing or decreasing. It can also be cyclical. When times are bad, for instance—think of the Great Recession of 2007 to 2009—discounters tend to do well. Put another way, customers' WTP for more expensive products and services tends to decline. Once the economy picks up again, however, their WTP for more expensive items tends to rise again, and, as a result, the contributed values of the "up-market" stores tend to rise again, too.

Assessing the Sustainability of Profits

Assuming that the pie is relatively stable (or increasing), there will be value to capture. But you still have to worry about whether you'll be the one doing the capturing—that is, whether your profits will persist. Answering this question depends, in part, on the source of your profitability. If your profits are due to value-gap advantages, then there are two ways you could lose your value-gap advantage: (1) existing players could increase their value gaps or (2) a new player with a larger value gap could enter the game.

· In the business strategy field, the first scenario is called a problem of imitation—that is, the possibility that another firm will be able to imitate whatever it is that gives your firm a larger value gap. The second scenario concerns a new firm's ease of entry. The question, then, is how you can limit imitation and/or entry through what the strategy field calls *barriers to entry*. In other words, the sustainability of your value-gap advantage can be reduced to the question of whether or not there are barriers to entry that protect it.

Let's return to the game in figure 5.1 for examples of what can happen if there are no barriers to entry. In figure 16.2, Firm 3, formerly profitable in just the Luxury segment, has figured out a way to lower its cost to $3.50. It now has the largest gap in all three segments. Firms 1 and 2 are no longer profitable. Without a "barrier" to keep Firm 3 from lowering its cost (while producing the same product), the profitability of the other two firms may not be sustainable.

Firm 2 has a similar concern with buyer WTP. In figure 16.3, Firm 1, formerly profitable in just the Retro segment, has managed to increase the quality of its product without raising its costs. This has increased buyer WTP in the Standard segment up to the level of Firm 2. (The Luxury segment doesn't care that Firm 1's product is better.) Firm 1 now wins customers in both the Standard and Retro segments. Firm 2, again, is no longer profitable. Without a "barrier" to keep Firm 1 from raising buyer WTP for Firm 1's products, Firm 2's profitability may not be sustainable.

As these two examples suggest, barriers to entry can exist on both the buyer side and the cost or supplier side. On the buyer side, barriers to entry are the reasons our customers' WTP for our products or services remains higher than their WTP for our competitors' products or services. Buyer-side barriers to entry, therefore, serve to maintain our WTP advantage. On the cost or supplier side, barriers to entry serve to

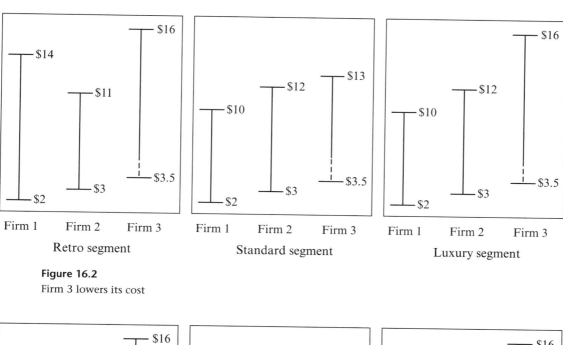

Figure 16.2
Firm 3 lowers its cost

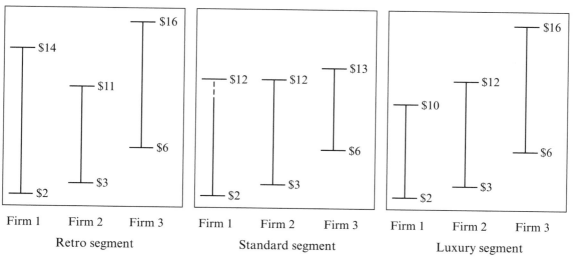

Figure 16.3
Firm 1 increases Standard segment WTP

keep our costs lower than our competitors' costs and our suppliers' costs lower than our competitors' suppliers' costs. In other words, supplier-side barriers to entry serve to maintain our cost or SC advantage.

Generally speaking, there are no *universal* barriers to entry; each is peculiar to the situation under study. That said, there are some general categories, or examples, that tend to occur across a broad range of circumstances, which you can see outlined below. I want to emphasize, though, that these are just examples. This is not a complete list, and keep in mind that situations exist in which even these examples do not provide a barrier to entry.

Common buyer-side barriers to entry include:

- buyer switching costs
- buyer search costs
- buyer habits
- branding

A buyer switching cost—that is, the cost a buyer would incur if she were to switch from your product to another—is all but self-explanatory. The cost of learning to use a new product or service is a typical example. A competitor's product may perform just as well as yours, but buyers' WTP for that product will remain lower if they believe switching costs are involved. Buying a smart phone using a different operating system incurs switching costs of this type, as does using a new accounting program for your computer, or even using the services of a new accountant. Almost all change involves some cost. Switching costs, however, aren't always as high as buyers presume; witness the speed with which email overcame mail. All that was required was a small change in the way a typical daily job was performed—that is, instead of using typewriters, writers simply turned to computer keyboards.

It is important to remember that for a firm to maintain its WTP advantage over potential entrants, buyers need only *believe* in the costs of switching to a competitor's product or service—whether or not those costs are actually as high as buyers imagine them to be.

Buyer search costs—the time and energy your customer would have to expend to find and select an alternative to transacting with you—are another form of switching costs. This is particularly true if the product you make, or the service you offer, contains an element of trust. For this reason, buyers will typically pay more for a building contractor or auto mechanic they have come to trust. Once again, though, it's important to remember that the WTP advantage of the auto mechanic, for instance, need be based on no more than the buyer's *belief* that the mechanic is more worthy of trust.

Habits are another buyer-side barrier to entry. If, over time, our customers have developed the habit of using our services or of buying our products, they may develop a higher WTP for our products and/or services. In fact, they may get to the point where they are so used to buying from us, that if they had to, they might actually pay more not to have to switch to another product. In such cases, buyers' habits would confer a WTP advantage on our firm that no new entrant could overcome, at least in the short term.

Branding—namely marketing efforts designed to increase buyer WTP for your products or services—can also create a WTP advantage for your company. But whether or not branding actually constitutes a barrier to entry is open to discussion. The argument in favor of branding goes like this. It takes both time and money to establish a brand, and once established, maintaining a brand is cheaper than creating a new one. Thus, companies with existing brands can "out-market" potential entrants for two reasons: they have a WTP advantage with their established brand, and their marketing campaigns deliver a bigger benefit for a given expenditure. Meanwhile, the argument against branding as a barrier to entry goes like this. Whatever you gain from having established a WTP advantage is wiped out by the marketing costs incurred to establish and maintain that advantage. In other words, it's a wash. Seen from this perspective, branding might enable you to profitably serve a certain buyer segment, but it won't prevent other firms from entering the same segment should they create a more effective branding strategy.

You don't really need to decide whether or not branding is a barrier to entry, but if you do want to debate the issue, you might consider the market for cola-flavored drinks. Most would agree that Coke and Pepsi have a WTP advantage over other colas, and that this advantage is based on both branding and habit. But is it the branding or the habit that discourages other companies from creating a branded, cola-flavored drink?

Common cost or supplier-side barriers to entry include:

- economies of scale
- exclusive access to a key resource
- patents
- causal ambiguity

Economies of scale are the best-known barrier to entry on the cost side. Such economies often provide a cost advantage and, if sufficiently large, can deter all but those competitors willing to make an enormous initial investment. Economies of scale also function as barriers to entry when the sheer volume of one or more firms' output allows them to enjoy cost advantages that no new entrant can hope to obtain. Typically, these occur as a result of some sort of fixed cost. Firms with higher output can spread that cost over more units, thus giving them a cost advantage over firms with lower output. For an economy of scale to be a barrier to entry, however, there must usually be additional factors at play. For instance, there should be a clear reason why a new entrant would not be able to operate at the same scale as the existing firms. Or if the size of the initial investment required to operate at (high volume) scale is part of the deterrent, there should be a reason why the potential entrant would not recoup that investment.

Access to materials can also serve as a barrier to entry. Exclusive access to a key resource, for instance, provides a clear cost advantage over potential entrants. Quite simply, if the entrant cannot obtain the key resource, its cost for that resource will be effectively infinite; in such a case, the entrant can't make a competitive product. The long-term viability of this type of barrier to entry is, however, highly questionable. When the incentives are large enough, businesses are quite good at finding alternate ways of making a product. Designing around (what is perceived to be) a key resource is just one such example. Patent protection works in a similar way. The exclusivity provides a clear cost advantage over potential entrants; yet firms get better every day at working around existing patents.

Another example of a supplier-side barrier to entry is causal ambiguity, which is a catch-all phrase for situations in which a firm is exceptionally successful at making something or providing a service, but the reason why they are able to do it—the cause of their success—is ambiguous. One of the most compelling examples of causal ambiguity in modern times was Toyota's production system. Car companies around the world spent a great deal of time and money trying to match Toyota's low cost and high-conformance quality, but without much success. Toyota, for reasons that remained unknown for a long time, was able to make more consistently reliable cars at a lower cost than anyone else could.

Competency can be another barrier to entry—one somewhat related to causal ambiguity. Notions of competency periodically appear in the strategy field—distinct competencies, core competencies, dynamic capabilities, and so on—but the exact nature of these competencies continues to elude researchers. Nonetheless, most agree that a competency, or special expertise, can confer a cost advantage. If the product or service you offer requires special abilities, then, when judging the sustainability of your firm's value gap, you'll want to know if, or how easily, other firms can acquire them. What's more, if your firm is especially good at producing a certain product, or especially good at offering a specific service, you don't even need to know *why* you have an advantage, as long as you do. In fact, it may be better that you don't because no potential competitor can attempt to duplicate an advantage that we can't even explain ourselves. Causal ambiguity, in other words, may be most effective as a barrier to entry when our *own understanding* of the causality is ambiguous.

The discussion above assumed that firms' profits are based on value-gap advantages. If profits are based on excess demand, either direct or indirect through market-price effects, the logic above still holds. If a new player enters, there is always the concern that the excess demand will disappear. If that happens, and if the new player's value gap is larger than yours, then your profits could disappear. So you'll still want to have barriers to prevent entry.

There is an additional concern in the excess-demand scenario: an existing player could add capacity and meet the excess demand. Without a value-gap advantage, your firm's profits would be at risk. You might ask why an existing player might do this? If the existing player has a significant value-gap advantage, then exploiting this advantage over a larger number of units might generate more profits than restricting supply would. Thus, relying on excess demand when your firm has no value-gap advantage requires that you be aware not only of new entrants, but also of existing players acting like new entrants.

It might seem that sustainability is more precarious when your profitability is based on excess demand rather than on value-gap advantages. I don't know of any empirical tests of this possibility, but it is worth emphasizing the following difference. When profits are due to a value-gap advantage, they come from both increasing the pie and stealing profits from competitors. Your value-gap advantage is a measure of the extent to which you increase the pie. And the fact that you win customers with this advantage means that some competitors lose customers. It's important to understand that for your value-gap advantage—and hence your profits—to disappear, another player would have to find a way to increase the pie even more. This may or may not be feasible. In contrast, when profits are due to excess demand, your firm's contributed value is based on the fact that the pie is smaller than it could be. For your profits to disappear, all it takes is another player increasing the pie to a size that is known to be feasible.

When the Pie Is Disappearing: A Broader View

When it appears that value will no longer be created—due to, say, dramatic innovations—the situation might seem hopeless, for without a pie, there can be no profits.

Granted, the situation *might* be hopeless, but there is one thought exercise that you should always try before assuming that the opportunity for value creation is completely gone. The key is to think in terms of demand for the underlying product—for example, transportation instead of the *means* used to transport people and goods. Using an historical example, let's say that you're in the business of making horse-drawn carriages and that the year is 1910—or two years after the first Model T rolled off the assembly line. Automobiles have been around for a while, and while ownership is still not widespread, you don't need a great deal of imagination to envision a time in which horses and the carriages they pull will no longer contribute much value in the transportation game. All is not lost, however, for while horse-drawn carriages are on the way out, the value created in the transportation game is rising rapidly. Put another way, buyers' WTP for transportation isn't shrinking—what's shrinking is their WTP for horse-drawn transportation. In this case, the question is whether your firm's skill set or means of production can be adapted to the new transportation market, even as the old market shrinks.

The wheels that your firm makes for horse-drawn carriages, for instance, could easily be adapted to automobiles. In the same way, those who upholster your carriages could easily adapt their skills to finishing the interiors of automobiles or to providing convertible tops much like those used on carriages. In this sense, you are simply identifying new businesses for your firm's products. The same is true for suppliers. Think of those who held the reins one hundred years ago—the teamsters—and how easily they were able to move from one technology to the next. While the carriage no longer needed a horse, it still needed a driver, and to further establish the connection, you need only consider that today's drivers still sit behind "beasts" measured in horsepower.

If the pie from which you derive your profits is shrinking, then it may help to focus on the underlying needs that each business satisfies. In the example above, the pie in the horse-drawn carriage business was declining, but the pie in the transportation business was growing. With this broader perspective, you may be able to identify a new way for your firm to contribute value—such as car interiors instead of carriage interiors.

When the pie is disappearing due to dramatically rising costs, it might seem that a broader perspective will not help. The survival of the pie will rely simply on finding a cheaper alternative for providing the product (or service). A broader perspective might nonetheless still help. For instance, suppose that you are in the business of providing fail-safe, offshore oil rigs, for example. Designing such a rig would appear to be financially infeasible. But a firm might be able to design an infallible early-warning, information system. Such a system would allow engineers to intervene before a failure occurred, thus effectively making the rig fail-safe. This approach is, in fact, used in many products, including passenger elevators.

Again, if the total value created is shrinking, it may be an inevitable consequence of progress or rising costs. But it is always worthwhile to think about both the underlying need for the product and the underlying function of the production process before making a final assessment about the sustainability of the pie.

17 Strategic Moves: Changing the Game

There are two ways a game can change: external factors can change it, and players can change it. In the previous chapter, we saw examples of both these ways. The question of whether or not the pie is sustainable is the question of whether external factors will change the game. In the case of a game with buyers, firms, and suppliers, for instance, buyers' willingnesses to pay and suppliers' costs are based on factors outside of the game. Any changes in these factors can, therefore, be viewed as external changes to the game.

While the sustainability of the total value created typically depends on external changes to the game, the sustainability of a firm's profits will typically depend on another player either not entering the game or not improving its value gap. Both of these actions—entering and improving—are *strategic moves*, which we define as purposeful actions that a player can take to change the game. In this chapter, we look at some of the more important strategic moves that occur in business contexts.

A Basic Strategic Decision

For an initial example, let's start with a decision about whether or not to compete for a new segment of buyers. Suppose that there are two firms and two buyer segments. Buyers in both segments have a WTP of $8 for Firm 2's product. However, the buyers in one of the segments—we'll call them Experienced Buyers—have a WTP of $12 for Firm 1's product, while the buyers in the other segment, or the Inexperienced Buyers, have a WTP of $6 for the same product. To illustrate, let's suppose that there are 1,000 buyers in each segment and that each buyer buys one new product every year. Finally, let's assume that each firm has the capacity to produce more than 1,000 units per year at a cost of $4 per unit (see figure 17.1).

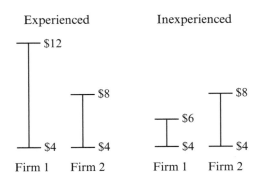

Figure 17.1
Initial game

If competition is unrestricted, Firm 1 can make $4,000 per year—its value-gap advantage in the Experienced segment. Similarly, Firm 2 can make $2,000 per year—its value-gap advantage in the Inexperienced segment.

Let's introduce a strategic decision—that is, a purposeful attempt to change the game. Suppose that by spending $20,000, Firm 1 can increase its capacity to more than 2,000 units per year. Moreover, for a one-time promotional expense of $8,000, Firm 1 can convince Inexperienced Buyers to try its product, thereby increasing that segment's WTP for its product from $6 to $12. In short, for a one-time expense of $28,000, Firm 1 can establish a value-gap advantage in *both* segments. Figure 17.2 depicts this strategic decision with a *decision tree*. The square box (called a *decision node*) represents the decision. Each line (a "branch" of the "tree") emanating from the decision node represents a possible choice. In this example, the top branch represents the decision to expand capacity and promote the product at a one-time cost of $28,000, while the bottom branch represents the decision to leave the game unchanged. At the end of each branch, we put the consequence of the choice.

The final step is to calculate the payoff for each option. Because each option involves a stream of payments, Firm 1 would typically compute the net present value (NPV) for each case. NPV calculations can get quite complicated, but since this is just an example, we'll use a standard approximation. First, we'll assume that the payments last for a very long time. Second, we'll assume that Firm 1 can borrow as much money as it wants at some fixed interest rate i. With these two assumptions, Firm 1's NPV for earnings of $4,000 per year would be $4,000/i$. Again, since this is just an example, we'll keep things simple and assume an interest rate of 10 percent. Thus, Firm 1's payoff for the case in which it does nothing is $4,000/0.10 = $40,000.

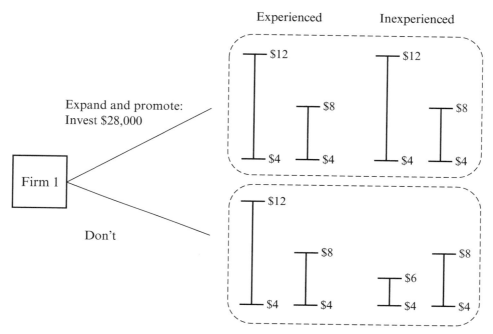

Figure 17.2
Strategic decision to change game

To compute the payoff for the case that Firm 1 chooses to expand and promote, we do a similar calculation. If it invests the $28,000, it will incur that cost in the first year. But it will then have a value-gap advantage in both segments and, from that point on, will make $8,000 a year. Using the same approximation as before, Firm 1 evaluates this stream of payments as $8,000/0.10 = $80,000. Thus, the payoff for the "expand and promote" option is $80,000 – $28,000 = $52,000. Figure 17.3 depicts our final representation of this strategic decision.

Most strategic decisions can be modeled this way, using the process above. We begin by identifying a specific strategy (e.g., changing the WTP of a particular segment by having buyers try our product), we then estimate the changes to the game that will result from the strategy (i.e., Inexperienced Buyers' WTP for our product will increase from $6 to $12), and, finally, we calculate the potential profitability in the new scenario. This process becomes especially useful when more than one player is considering a strategic move, but before I explain why, I'll provide a few more examples in which only one player has a strategic move.

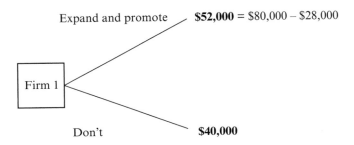

Figure 17.3
Strategic decision with payoffs

Price-Setting as a Strategic Move

Throughout this book, I have treated prices as a consequence of competition and bargaining. Implicit in this approach is the assumption that the game is fixed. Prices may change as a consequence of competition and bargaining, but these changes in prices do not change the game itself. But there are times when prices do, in fact, change the game. For instance, consider a firm's decision to offer an "introductory low price." If this attracts new buyers, and these new buyers have a higher WTP after trying the firm's products, then the game has changed. In such a case, the offer an introductory low price is a strategic move. In fact, in figure 17.3, the strategic move to "promote" could just as easily have been a strategic move to offer an introductory low price.

Another example of pricing as a strategic move is when price is used as a signal of quality. This could even be thought of as an "introductory high price." If the quality of a new product is unknown, a firm could choose a high price for the product launch, thus signaling that the new product is a premium product. If the high price increases the WTP of some buyers, then the game will have changed—the introductory high price would be a strategic move.

Because prices typically reflect the effects of competition and bargaining, the approach in this book has been to treat prices as a consequence in the given game. But as the introductory price examples show, there are times when the choice of a price should be viewed as a strategic move that changes the game.

Barriers to Entry: Entry as a Bad Move for a Competitor

In the previous chapter, I discussed how the sustainability of a firm's profits is usually justified with a barrier-to-entry story—the sustainability of a firm's profits depending on another player—the "entrant"—either not entering the game or not improving its value gap. Let's see how we can view barriers to entry from a strategic-move perspective.

With barriers to entry—as described in the previous chapter—you want one of two conditions to hold. If your profits are due to value-gap advantages, you don't want another firm to be able to duplicate or improve on your value gap in your buyer segments. And if your profits are due to excess demand, you don't want another firm to enter, where entry could be actual entry or expansion of existing capacity.

If we describe these two conditions from the decision-making perspective of a competitor, the competitor has two options: *Enter* or *Don't enter.* (We will use "enter" in a general sense here. It will include duplicating our value gap as well as entering with additional capacity.) Quite simply, if there is a barrier to entry, the consequences of the *Don't enter* choice look better to a competitor than the consequences of entering. This decision is easy to describe verbally, but for more complicated decisions, it can be useful to use a decision tree. Figure 17.4 provides the decision tree.

In figure 17.4, we describe the payoffs verbally. The figure emphasizes that the logic behind a barrier to entry must yield the following fact: the resulting profits from entry, net of the cost of entry, make the competitor worse off. This can be due to the fact that the incremental profits from entry are zero—for instance, the entrant is not able to get a value-gap advantage. It also can be due to the fact that the incremental profits are less than the cost of entry—for instance, there might not be enough demand to cover the initial cost of a factory. Or it can be a combination of the two. If you look back at chapter 16, you'll see that all of the barrier-to-entry examples fit into these three categories.

Entry and Strategic Change

A firm's decision to change its strategy—which includes decisions to enter a new market—has the same structure as the *Enter* vs. *Don't Enter* decision (see figure 17.5).

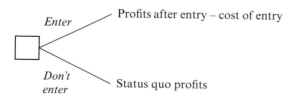

Figure 17.4
Potential entrant's decision

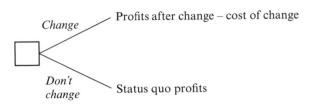

Figure 17.5
Strategic change decision

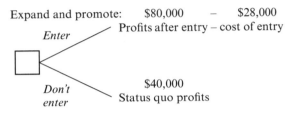

Figure 17.6
Figure 17.3 revisited

The challenge in assessing this decision lies in understanding the incremental and status quo profits—which has been the main focus of this book. To assess the change, you have to assess what your profitability will be in the new scenario. To assess the status quo profits, your main concern will be the sustainability of those profits.

The first example in this chapter had this very structure. The "Change" move was to expand and promote. In figure 17.6, I put the specific details of figure 17.3 above the labels in figure 17.5.

Strategic Change and Uncertainty

In the above examples, there is an implicit assumption that the consequences of a strategic change are predictable. In fact, this is often not the case. To show how uncertainty would enter a decision, we consider a simple re-positioning example.

In the status quo scenario, we have a firm serving a niche segment of buyers and a competitor serving a broad segment, as depicted in figure 17.7. Assume that each firm has plenty of capacity and that the broad segment has 500 buyers and the niche segment has 100 buyers. If each firm captures its value-gap advantage, then the firm's status quo profit is $300.

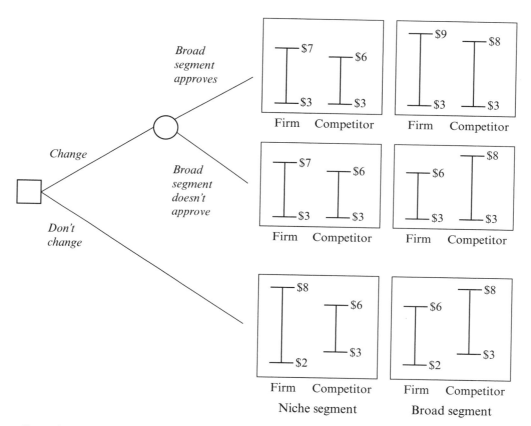

Figure 17.7
Uncertain strategic change

In this example, the firm is considering changing its product to appeal to the broad segment. While the firm is sure that the niche customers will still prefer its product—though not by as much—it is unsure whether the modified product will appeal to the broad segment.

For simplicity, we assume that there are only two scenarios: a broad buyer's WTP for the modified product either increases to $9 or stays at $6. In a decision tree, a small circle (called a *chance* node) depicts an uncertainty, and each branch emanating from the chance node is a possible outcome from the uncertainty. Assuming, again, that each firm captures its value-gap advantage, we can compute the profit for each scenario. Figure 17.8 summarizes the decision.

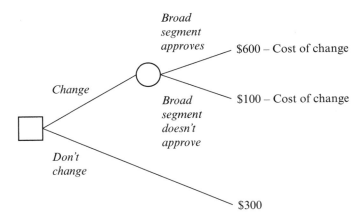

Figure 17.8
Uncertain strategic change—payoffs

   To decide what to do, the firm must assess the likelihood that the broad segment will like the modified product. If the firm is confident that the modified product will be a success, and if the cost of the modification is less than the incremental profit—$300— then the firm will change its product. At the other extreme, pessimism about the broad segment's approval or a large cost of modification will lead the firm to stay with the status quo. For situations between these two extremes, the firm has a more difficult decision.

Creating Competition, Part 1

Decisions about what products to offer or what markets to enter are basic strategic decisions. Another type of basic strategic move is the creation of competition—more precisely, competition for your firm. This decision happens all the time. For instance, when a real estate broker tries to get multiple buyers interested in a property, he is creating buyer competition. When a firm develops relationships with more than one supplier, it is often trying to create supplier competition. In fact, this might not seem to be much of a decision after all: if you can create competition for your firm, why wouldn't you?

   Unless you already have excess demand, you probably would always want to create buyer competition if there were a cost-effective way to do so. But whether or not to create supplier competition is less clear. For instance, consider your key employees. Do you want them believing that you are always looking for other people who could take

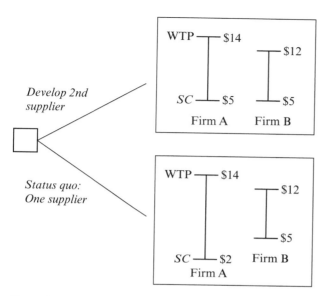

Figure 17.9
Supplier competition versus supplier coordination

their place? Your answer to this question probably depends on what business you are in, so let's consider the example in figure 17.9.

Firm A is choosing between two scenarios. In both scenarios, there is just one buyer. In the status quo scenario, there is only one supplier. Firm A is able to coordinate with the supplier, and, as a consequence, the supplier can serve it for $3 less than its cost for serving Firm B. Firm A has a value-gap advantage of $5, which will be split among Firm A, the supplier, and the buyer. So, in the bottom branch, Firm A's profit will be between zero and $5.

If Firm A chooses to work with an additional supplier, there will be buyer competition, but Firm A will have less time to coordinate with the original supplier. Consequently, both the original supplier and the additional supplier will have the same supplier cost for serving either firm. Firm A's value-gap advantage will be $2, which will be split between Firm A and the buyer. In the top branch, then, Firm A's profit will be between zero and $2.

Depending on how the bargaining is resolved, Firm A could choose not to develop supplier competition. For instance, if the buyer pays the same price in both situations, and if Firm A captures some of the coordination gains, then Firm A will prefer not to create supplier competition. Figure 17.10 depicts such a situation in which the buyer

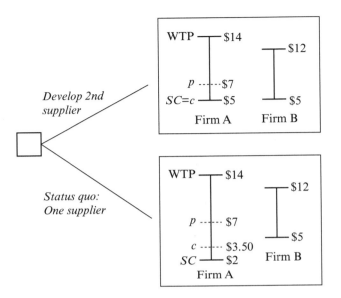

Figure 17.10
Choosing not to create supplier competition

captures only its guaranteed profit in both scenarios. Despite the compelling intuition behind creating competition, Firm A would choose not to do so in this situation.

Creating Competition, Part 2

The intuition for creating competition for suppliers and buyers is straightforward. Because competition will reduce their contributed values, a firm will typically be in a better position to capture more of the value created. For a similar reason, it might seem obvious that you would not want to create competition for yourself. In other words, you would not want to encourage competitors to enter your market. But there is at least one kind of situation in which you might be happy to have more competitors. When the presence of competitors will bring more buyers into the game and increase the pie, the advantages from increasing the pie can outweigh the disadvantages of increased competition from other firms.

Classic examples of this kind of situation include stores locating near each other to create a shopping district or restaurants locating near each other to create a dining district. For a more modern example, consider Google's decision to make its Android operating system open source versus Apple's decision not to. Google is betting that the benefits from increasing the pie will exceed any costs of encouraging competition. Apple, historically, has made the opposite bet.

Interaction of Strategic Moves

In the examples so far, we have given only one player a strategic move. This is often useful for understanding a firm's entry and positioning decisions, but there are situations in which you'll be interested in the interaction effects of strategic moves. For instance, if one player enters a market, will another one enter? Although we will consider the interaction between strategic moves, it is important to remember that this is not the only interaction in a game. When we look at any consequence of unrestricted competition, we are looking at a consequence of unrestricted, competitive interactions. Unrestricted competition, in fact, describes the interactions *within* a game. Strategic moves describe the interactions in choosing *between* games.

We'll start with an example in which two firms have a strategic move. Each firm has the capacity to produce more than 1,000 units per year at a cost of $2 per unit. There is just one segment of 1,000 buyers, and each buyer has a WTP of $5 for either firm's product. Figure 17.11 depicts the initial situation. Note that neither player has any contributed value, so neither firm will make any money.

Let's now suppose that each firm has the option to develop a new, improved product. To develop such a product, a firm would have to incur a one-time expense of $20,000, but the buyers' WTP for the new product would rise to $8—$3 more than their WTP for the current product. (Strictly for simplicity, we'll assume that the cost for the new product is still $2 per unit.) Since either firm can choose to develop a new product, we have to consider four scenarios: neither firm develops a new product, only Firm 1 develops a new product, only Firm 2 develops a new product, or both firms develop a new product. These four scenarios are depicted in figure 17.12.

Figure 17.12 is an example of an *outcome matrix*. When describing a situation in which two players have strategic moves, an outcome matrix describes all the possible outcomes. The rows of such a matrix depict one player's moves, and the columns depict the other player's moves. In figure 17.12, Firm 1's choice—that is, to maintain the status quo or to innovate—corresponds to a choice of row. For instance, Firm 1's choice to improve its product is depicted by the bottom two boxes. Similarly, Firm 2's choice corresponds to a choice of column. The left-hand column, for instance, depicts the two possible outcomes of Firm 2's decision to leave its product unchanged.

Sometimes an outcome matrix demonstrates the strategic essence of a situation without any further calculations, and this is the case with the game in figure 17.12. If

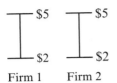

Figure 17.11
Initial situation

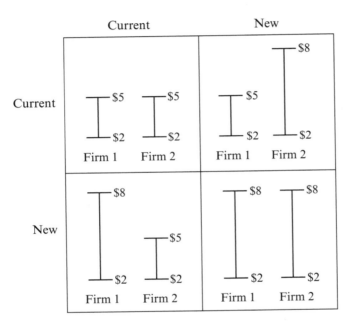

Figure 17.12
Outcome matrix

neither firm develops a new product, neither firm makes any money. If just one of the firms develops a new product, it will achieve a value-gap advantage and be able to profit. If, however, both firms choose to develop a new product, they will recreate a situation in which neither makes any money. Moreover, they will spend $20,000 doing it!

Figure 17.12 provides a qualitative summary of the possible outcomes, but to better understand what the players might choose to do, there are two more steps. We must quantify each outcome for each player, and we must account for the fact that one firm might be able to make its choice before the other. To quantify each outcome, let's assume (as we did in figure 17.3) that each buyer makes just one purchase every year. Thus, if one firm develops a new product, it will have a value-gap advantage of $3 and make $3,000 a year. As before, we'll assume that each firm views $3,000 a year as equivalent to a one-time payment of $30,000. The choice to develop the new product will give the firm a gain of $30,000 minus a development cost of $20,000, for a net gain of $10,000. But if both firms develop a new product, both will lose $20,000. Finally, if a firm chooses not to develop a new product, it neither gains nor loses, so we will assign it a payoff of zero. Figure 17.13 provides each player's payoff for each outcome. (Within each box, the left-hand number is Firm 1's payoff, and the right-hand number is Firm 2's payoff.)

Now that we know each player's payoff in each outcome, we can consider who moves when. Let's suppose that Firm 1 moves first. Call this *Game 17.1*. Firm 1 will choose whether or not to develop the new product. Firm 2 will then have the same choice. Interestingly, if Firm 2 anticipates what it might do before Firm 1 moves, it actually has four strategies: (1) it can develop the new product no matter what Firm 1 chooses, (2) it can stay with the current product no matter what Firm 1 chooses, (3) it can develop the new product only if Firm 1 develops the new product, or (4) it can develop the new product only if Firm 1 does not. To describe this game, it is convenient to use a decision tree. Figure 17.14 shows the tree, but notice that because more than one player has a decision to make, we now call it a game tree.

In figure 17.14, the left-hand payoff corresponds to Firm 1's payoff, and the right-hand payoff corresponds to Firm 2's payoff. From the figure we can see that Firm 2 will develop the new product only if Firm 1 does not. (This was strategy 4 above.) Knowing this, Firm 1 would then choose to develop the new product. To make Firm 1's decision easier to see, you can cross out the moves that Firm 2 would not take. Figure 17.15 illustrates this. You can see that based on what Firm 2 would do, Firm 1 has a choice

	Current	New
Current	0, 0	0, 10
New	10, 0	−20, −20

Figure 17.13
Outcome matrix with payoffs

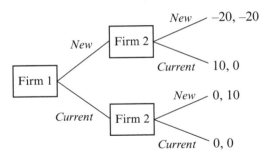

Figure 17.14
Game 17.1 game tree

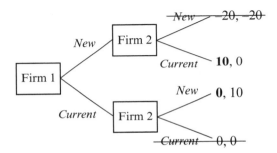

Figure 17.15
Firm 1's decision, given Firm 2's move

between $10,000 from developing the new product and zero from staying with the current product. If I have estimated the payoff correctly, you should be able to predict what should happen: only Firm 1 develops the new product.

Now if you believed that Firm 2 would be the first to decide, you would have a different game, and you would draw the tree differently. You would have Firm 2 making the first decision, and the analysis would yield the opposite conclusion: only Firm 2 would develop the product. In general, how you draw the tree will depend on your assessment of who moves when. Figure 17.14 depicts a relatively simple scenario: Firm 1 moves first, and Firm 2 sees what Firm 1 decides. But it may be the case that Firm 2 doesn't know what Firm 1 decided or, for that matter, whether Firm 1 even made a decision. I won't go into these more complicated scenarios, but there is one that we should discuss: the players choose simultaneously. Call this *Game 17.2*. Unfortunately, there is no known game tree for this situation, so I'll use what is called a *game matrix*. Figure 17.6 depicts the game matrix for *Game 17.2*.

	Current	New
Current	0, 0	0, 10
New	10, 0	−20, −20

Figure 17.16
Game matrix for *Game 17.2*

You'll notice that this game matrix looks exactly like the outcome matrix in figure 17.13. This can be confusing, but here is the point to remember: if players move simultaneously, the outcome matrix and the game matrix will be the same. Note that in this example, if the players move simultaneously, it is much harder to predict what will happen. When one player moved first, we could deduce what should happen. But now, anything could happen. Both players could develop the new product because each believes that the other will not. This is the lower right scenario. Both could stay with the current product because each believes that the other is developing the new product. This is the upper left scenario. Or we could have one of the other two scenarios. Note, though, that in the other two scenarios, both players are correct in their beliefs. For instance, in the lower left scenario, Firm 1 is choosing to develop the new product because it believes (correctly) that Firm 2 will not. And Firm 2 is choosing not to develop because it believes (correctly) that Firm 1 is. In contrast, in the scenarios in which both firms developed or both firms stayed with the current product, the firms were wrong in their beliefs. In this scenario, having incorrect beliefs led to outcomes that were worse than the outcomes based on correct beliefs. The outcome (−20, −20) is strictly worse than (0, 10) and (10, 0); the outcome (0, 0) is weakly worse than (0, 10) and (10, 0). When we have an outcome that is worse than an outcome that is possible with correct beliefs, we say that we have *coordination failure*.

Coordination & Management: An Example of Shaping Beliefs

Coordination—and the possibility that it will not occur—plays a central role in value creation. In the game in figure 17.16, coordination failure may have seemed highly likely. In each of the two coordinated outcomes, only one of the firms benefited. So, if each firm had self-serving beliefs—that is, if each firm believed that the other would not develop the new product—coordination failure would be inevitable. In this section, we'll consider a less insidious coordination game. As before, we'll consider a game in which two firms have the choice to innovate or not.

In *Game 17.3*, the firms make an identical product, and each firm has the capacity to produce up to 1,000 units per year at a cost of $2 per unit. In this example, we will assume that there is excess demand for the product: there are more than 2,000 buyers, each with a WTP of $6 for either firm's product. Each firm can choose to develop a new product at a one-time cost of $15,000. There is one complication, though. A buyer's WTP for the new product will increase only if *both* firms choose to develop it. If only one of the firms develops the new product, a buyer's WTP will remain at $6 for either firm's product. But if both firms develop the new product, each buyer's WTP will jump to $9 for either firm's product. Consider an example: suppose that a computer manufacturer has the ability to introduce a faster operating system. If other manufacturers don't adopt the same system, developers will have little incentive to create new applications for it. If buyers perceive the limited choice of apps to be a weakness of the system, their WTP for computers that use it will not increase—*unless* they believe that other manufacturers will also choose the new operating system. Figure 17.17 depicts the outcome matrix for *Game 17.*3

To compute the payoffs for each scenario in figure 17.17, start with the scenario in which neither firm develops the new product. Since there is excess demand, each firm will capture its full value gap for its entire capacity, which implies an annual profit of $4,000. Let's assume that each firm views an annual stream of $4,000 payments as equivalent to a one-time payment of $40,000. Thus, if neither firm adopts the new system, each firm receives a payoff of $40,000.

If just one firm adopts the system, each firm will continue to have profits of $4,000 per year. But the adopting firm will have the innovation cost of $15,000. This implies a payoff of $25,000 for the adopting firm and $40,000 for the non-adopting firm.

Finally, if both firms adopt the new system, each will now have profits of $7,000 per year. Adjusting for the costs of adoption, this implies a payoff of $55,000 for each firm. We will assume that the firms move simultaneously, so figure 17.18 depicts both the outcome matrix and the game matrix.

In this game, unlike the game in figure 17.16, the best outcome for each player is also the best outcome for both players: if both players choose to adopt the new system, they both make as much money as possible ($55,000 each). Furthermore, this outcome is entirely possible. If Firm 1 believes that Firm 2 will adopt, it will adopt as well. Similarly, if Firm 2 believes that Firm 1 will adopt, it will adopt too. Because this best

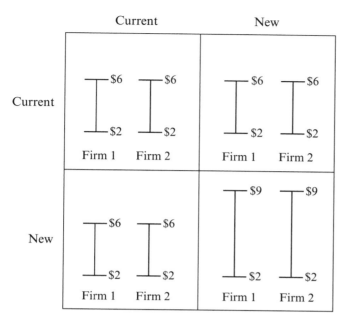

Figure 17.17
Game 17.3 outcome matrix

	Current	New
Current	40, 40	40, 25
New	25, 40	55, 55

Figure 17.18
Game 17.3 game matrix (and outcome matrix)

outcome is possible with correct beliefs, we will have coordination failure if any other outcome occurs. Is another outcome possible? Sadly, "yes." Suppose that Firm 1 believes that Firm 2 *won't* adopt. In that case, according to the game matrix, Firm 1 shouldn't adopt either. The same is true for Firm 2. If Firm 1 doesn't adopt, Firm 2 shouldn't either. Both firms would be acting optimally, given their beliefs, and their decisions would lead to inferior outcomes for *everyone*. Both firms would make less money, and buyers wouldn't have the chance to buy a better product. We have coordination failure.

Even more frustrating is that coordination failure doesn't have to happen. As I noted above, as long as each firm believes that the other is going to adopt, it will adopt too. We use the term "coordination failure" precisely because there is a plausible scenario in which both players will be better off. The failure, therefore, is actually a failure of belief, and if the firms' beliefs could be changed, the "failure" could be avoided.

This shaping of beliefs is one of the central responsibilities of management. Consider this micro-level example of *Game 17.3*. At the conclusion of a meeting, everyone agrees to collaborate on a new project, and everyone leaves the meeting intending to do his or her share. No one ends up doing anything, however, because each player *believes* that no one else will follow through and so decides not to waste his or her time. (This outcome is shown in the upper left-hand box in figure 17.18.) It is management's job, therefore, to make sure that everyone leaves the meeting *believing* that everyone else will do his or her job.

A mid-level example might involve different departments within the same company failing to coordinate the implementation of a new initiative—for example, a process-improvement program. A macro-level example might occur in the marketplace, where software developers fail to write programs for a new operating system because they believe that other developers won't write programs, or where companies decide not to invest because they believe that other companies will not invest. All of these examples of coordination failure have the same strategic structure as *Game 17.3*, and the re-shaping of beliefs could prevent all of these failures.

Incentives and Externalities

Why, once again, should management—whether it is responsible for a single department, divisions within a company, or companies within a sector—take the lead in preventing coordination failure? The answer, quite simply, is that the *possibility* of coordination failure is omnipresent. To make this point, we need to consider two problems that can affect almost any business decision.

The first is the alignment of incentives with preferred outcomes. No matter the business, management uses incentives to convince employees to work toward the company's goals. Management may, for example, offer incentives to the assembly-line shift that produces the most products with the fewest defects. From a value-creation perspective, incentive alignment is defined as follows: incentives are aligned if, when a firm makes a strategic move that increases its contributed value, its profits also increase. This should make sense by now because profits, from the perspective of value creation and competition, *should* be based on contributed value. The first goal, then, is to ensure that if a player changes the game in a way that increases his contributed value, his captured value will increase as well.

The second problem is that of externalities. Loosely put, our second goal is to ensure that we—or any other players—have no effect on value creation in which we are not involved. Consider the following example. Suppose that one of your competitors serves a customer segment you are not interested in serving. If you spread rumors that the competitor's product is flawed, a buyer's WTP for the competitor's product may decline, which, in turn, would lead to a reduction in the total value created. Because you are not involved in the transactions between your competitor and his customers, your negative effect is considered an externality. Or, in the corporate sphere, suppose that one division of your company does something to hurt the entire company's reputation, affecting the way customers of the other divisions view the company's products or services. Since the division responsible for the change in customer sentiment across the company was not involved in the other divisions' businesses, the negative effect would, again, be considered an externality.

If incentives are aligned, and if we can prevent externalities, then any player's strategic moves that change the game favorably for him will also change it favorably for everyone else—that is, the total value created in the game will increase. In a corporation, it follows that strategic moves increasing one division's profits will increase the corporation's profits too. And in the economy at large, every time a player changes the game to increase his profits, the value created in the economy as a whole increases as well.

You might wonder if I just described the conditions necessary for the operation of Adam Smith's famous invisible hand. As long as we can align incentives and prevent externalities, will self-interested behavior lead to the biggest pie for all? The answer, unfortunately, is no, owing to the possibility of coordination failure (the adoption game of *Game 17.3* was an example of this). Therefore, if you want Adam Smith's invisible hand to work, you need to ensure that coordination failure won't occur.

And that leads to an even more important result. Suppose that you have incentive alignment and that there is no risk of an externality problem. And suppose further that you are in an interactive situation, one in which your choice of action depends on what you think others will do. Whenever this is the case, there is a chance of coordination failure. And that is why I said that the possibility of coordination failure is omnipresent, and that management's willingness to take responsibility is so important.

This is far from just a theoretical construct. If you're involved in the sort of typical decision-making that goes on in today's business world, where your decisions are based, in part, on what you think others will do, then there's a very good chance that you will have to address coordination failure.

So, someone must be responsible for coordination. In a company, management is clearly that "someone." When we consider macroeconomic environments, though, the identity of the "someone" is not so clear. We quickly encounter a fundamental difference of opinion between those who believe that the market should manage itself, and those who believe in some form of governmental management. What cannot be disputed, however, is that coordination failure is always a *possibility*.

Appendix: Game Matrices for Game Trees

Because there is no game tree for a simultaneous-move game, I use a game matrix for such games. But this does not imply that a game matrix always represents a simultaneous-move game. In this appendix, I will construct the game matrix for *Game 17.1*, shown again in figure 17.19.

To construct a game matrix, I need to identify each player's strategy. A player's strategy has to indicate what move it will take at any decision node it might reach, even if

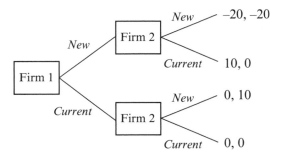

Figure 17.19
Game 17.1 game tree

it doesn't believe that it will reach that node. Fortunately, we have already identified each player's strategies. Firm 1 has only two: develop or don't develop the new product. Firm 2 has four: (1) it can develop the new product no matter what Firm 1 chooses, (2) it can stay with the current product no matter what Firm 1 chooses, (3) it can develop the new product only if Firm 1 develops the new product, or (4) it can develop the new product only if Firm 1 does not.

Note that each of the four strategies merely states what Firm 2 will do at its two decision nodes. (In figure 17.19, we see that Firm 2 has a "top" and "bottom" decision node.) Table 17.1 shows how the verbal descriptions of Firm 2's strategies correspond to the moves in the tree.

Having identified each player's strategies, constructing the matrix is straightforward. Set up two rows, one for each of Firm 1's strategies, and four columns, one for each of Firm 2's strategies. Then in each cell, put the payoffs that correspond to what would happen if Firm 1 chose the strategy corresponding to the cell's row and if Firm 2 chose the strategy corresponding to the cell's column. Figure 17.20 provides the game matrix for this example.

If you recall the analysis of the game tree, Firm 1 would develop the new product and Firm 2 would not. This corresponds to the upper right-hand cell of the game matrix: Firm 1 choosing the "New" strategy and Firm 2 choosing the "Develop if Firm

Table 17.1

	Description	Top node choice	Bottom node choice
1	Develop always	New	New
2	Current always	Current	Current
3	Develop if Firm 1 develops	New	Current
4	Develop if Firm 2 doesn't	Current	New

	New, New	Current, Current	New, Current	Current, New
New	−20, −20	10, 0	−20, −20	10, 0
Current	0, 10	0, 0	0, 0	0, 10

Figure 17.20
Game 17.1 game matrix

1 Doesn't" strategy. You can see this conclusion directly in the game matrix. By looking at the "New" row, you'll see that if Firm 1 chooses to develop the new product, the best that Firm 2 can do is 0. This happens if it chooses strategy 2 or 4. By looking at the "Current" row, you'll see that if Firm 1 does not develop the new product, the best that Firm 2 can do is 10. This happens if it chooses strategy 1 or 4. Thus, strategy 4—the far right column—is the best choice for Firm 2, *no matter what* Firm 1 does. (A game theorist would say that strategy 4 is a *dominant* strategy for Firm 2.) Turning to Firm 1, if Firm 2 chooses the far right column, Firm 1 will choose the upper row—the "New" strategy. Thus, the outcome will be 10 for Firm 1 and 0 for Firm 2, just as we saw in the game tree.

18 Strategic Moves: Restrictions

This book focuses on how to be profitable if competition is unrestricted. You have to be better—identify customer segments in which you have a value-gap advantage—or you have to be needed—there must be excess demand for your products. If neither is the case, then two different conditions must be satisfied for you to be profitable—competition must be restricted, and the restrictions must allow you to make money.

Unfortunately, there is no general theory of restrictions to competition. If you are in a situation in which competition is restricted, there are no guidelines for being profitable. Instead, you have to look at the specifics of the situation and analyze whether or not you can be profitable. Fortunately, I have shown you something that can help you perform this analysis—the game tree. Think about what you might do, what your competitors and other relevant players might do, and construct a game tree. Because this requires you to make many judgments, constructing a game tree is more art than science. For illustration, I'll present three examples, each showing how a firm with zero contributed value might be profitable. The main purpose of these examples is to demonstrate the method of using game trees to model situations with restricted competition. But these examples describe situations that often reoccur, so they are interesting in their own right, as well.

Example: Competition Restricted due to Firm Choices

We'll use the same setup as the initial game of figure 17.11. There are two firms, each with the capacity to produce more than 1,000 units per year at a cost of $2 per unit. There is just one segment of 1,000 buyers, and each buyer has a WTP of $5 for either firm's product. Further, each buyer will buy one unit every year. Figure 18.1 depicts this setup. Unlike *Game 17.1*, though, neither firm has the ability to improve its product.

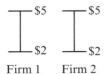

Firm 1   Firm 2

Figure 18.1
Initial situation: zero profits under unrestricted competition

	Maintain	Compete
Maintain	15000, 15000	0, 2950
Compete	2950, 0	0, 0

Figure 18.2
Game matrix: competition restricted due to firm choices

Each firm has a contributed value of zero. With unrestricted competition, each firm will make no money every year.

Let's introduce a restriction. Suppose that each firm agrees to hold out for a price of $5 per unit. Note that with unrestricted competition, this is not sustainable. If both firms are trying to get the same price, sales will probably be split somehow between the two firms. But then one firm could lower price slightly, say to $4.95, and serve all the buyers. So, for our restriction, we suppose that the two firms will agree to maintain a price of $5. Implicitly, this would be an agreement not to compete as aggressively.

With this agreement, each firm would make $1,500 per year, assuming that they split the customer base evenly. You might ask if such an agreement is credible. This is a good question and not an easy one to answer. The history of cartels is, in part, a history of when such agreements are and are not credible. But there is a standard story that economists tell about how it can be credible, so let's look at it.

Suppose that each firm has the choice to either maintain a price of $5 or to compete. If it competes, it will drop its price as much as necessary to win all the customers. If we further assume than once a firm chooses to compete, the other firm will compete as well, we can construct a simultaneous-move game in which the $5 price is credible. Figure 18.2 shows a game matrix for such a game. The payoffs assume that a profit of $1,500 per year is valued the same as a one-time profit of $15,000. Thus, as you can see from the matrix, the one-time benefit of making $2,950 once is not as good as the benefit of $1,500 per year over time. We have a story in which the restriction to competition is credible and in which firms with zero contributed value are profitable.

Example: Competition Restricted due to Law or Social Convention

In this next example, we do not have firms choosing to compete less aggressively. Instead, we have firms that are restricted in how they bargain with customers. Due to either a law or a social convention, a firm must offer all its customers the same price. Given this restriction, suppose that there are two firms, A and B. Firm A can produce 100 units at a cost of $2 per unit. Firm B can produce ten units at a cost of $2.50 per unit. There are 100 buyers, each willing to pay either $6 for Firm A's product or $5.50 for Firm B's product; see figure 18.3.

Firm B clearly contributes zero value, both qualitatively and quantitatively. It has higher costs, and its product is perceived to be inferior. With unrestricted competition, Firm B will make no money, and the presence of Firm B will limit Firm A's profit to, at most, $1 per unit—its value-gap advantage.

But competition is not unrestricted. Suppose that Firm B is selling its product for $4 per unit. At that price, a buyer would capture $1.50. Now consider Firm A's strategic decision. If it wants to be sure to win all 100 buyers, it would have to make sure that all buyers capture at least $1.50. Because Firm A is perceived to have a better product, a price of $4.49 would suffice, giving Firm A a profit of $249 (assuming that Firm B does not lower price). But Firm A could also ignore the fact that Firm B can serve ten buyers. Instead, it could offer a higher price, say, $5.50, knowing that it would sell only 90 units. But 90 units at a price of $5.50 yields a profit of $315 (see figure 18.4). Firm A does better in this second scenario. More important, Firm B makes a profit in this second scenario.

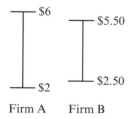

Firm A   Firm B

Figure 18.3
Initial situation: Firm B's profit is zero under unrestricted competition

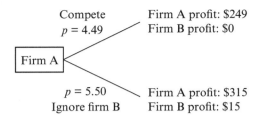

Figure 18.4
Game tree: competition restricted due to one-price requirement

On the surface, there is a simple explanation for this example. Firm B is so small that it is not worthwhile for Firm A to compete with it. But the subtlety lies in the "not worthwhile" part of the explanation. If Firm A could offer a different price to different customers, then it would compete with Firm B over Firm B's ten customers but then offer a higher price to the remaining buyers. This could happen if competition were unrestricted, but it is not. In particular, Firm A must offer the same price to all buyers. As a result, Firm B is able to make a profit.

Example: Competition Restricted due to Lack of Information

Our final restriction example is similar to the previous one. A firm with no contributed value is able to make a profit because its competitors ignore it. But in this case, ignoring it is not by strategic choice; rather, competitors literally do not know about it. This might seem like a trivial case. Saying that you can make money because more capable competitors don't know about you doesn't seem to be a particularly profound insight. But for an entrepreneur, it can be a useful point to remember.

Suppose that you are an entrepreneur with a product that you believe will someday give you a significant value-gap advantage. But being a realist, you know that in the short term, you are at a disadvantage. (Perhaps you still have some design issues and haven't driven production costs down as far as you plan to.) In these early stages, competition is not your friend. If you can find customer segments in which your competitors are likely not to learn about you, so much the better. Or, if not, if you can find markets where restrictions might make it costly for competitors to compete with you, as in the previous example—that would be good, too. Either way, a key part of understanding profitability is understanding that restrictions to competition can work in your favor.

Conclusion: A Coherent Story

Business strategy is a curious notion. For millennia, people have successfully transacted business, so it is not at all obvious that we need a field called "business strategy." Given this long and successful history, is it reasonable to believe that we can add anything to the practice of business?

Alternatively, business is frighteningly, almost hopelessly complex. In particular, when business is transacted in a competitive environment, it is highly interactive. And the interactions are between impossibly unpredictable entities—that is, human beings. Given all this complexity, we can ask the same question again, although for different reasons: Is it reasonable to believe that we can add anything to the practice of business?

The answer is "yes." We can make sure that there is a coherent story for a firm's profitability. By a coherent story, I mean a story with two characteristics—it is logically consistent, and it is consistent with the businessperson's honest assessment of the situation he faces.

This book provides a logically consistent framework within which you can generate your own coherent story about your own business. If you combine the theory in this book with your best business judgment, you will be as prepared as possible for the inevitable complexity of the modern business environment. And keep in mind that sound business judgment is not just incidental to sound theory—it is essential to making the theory work. In fact, the theory *requires* it. What are some of the judgments you need to make? You have to decide who views you as a competitor, and whether they will react to your moves in the market. You have to figure out how your customers view you, especially in relation to your competitors. You have to determine how your suppliers view doing business with you. There are no easy answers, but then again, there shouldn't be. Any advice that doesn't require you to make these judgments—that is, that doesn't respect your knowledge of your own business—is superficial at best.

But, if you make these judgments, the path to understanding profitability is straightforward:

1. Identify which players are relevant to your business.

2. Assess whether you can be profitable under unrestricted competition:

Can you identify segments in which you have a value-gap advantage?

If not, is there excess demand?

3. Test the assumption that competition is unrestricted: Is your assessment from step 2 consistent with current or predicted profitability?

4. Check for sustainability of profits:

If competition is unrestricted, is the pie sustainable? Are there barriers to entry?

If competition is restricted, will the restrictions enabling (or interfering with) your profits continue to be in place?

5. Consider changing the status quo:

If competition only partially determines prices, can you negotiate for more?

Are there beliefs to be shaped?

Or is changing the game the only way to change your firm's profits?

To make these five steps clear, this book started with the theory of profitability under unrestricted competition. I always recommend that an analysis begin with an assumption of unrestricted competition, for two reasons. First, that scenario is consistent with classical supply and demand and, thus, with most people's intuitive understanding of competition. Second, unrestricted competition is the most demanding baseline. If your business can be profitable under unrestricted competition, then you have as solid a foundation for profitability as is economically possible.

One fortuitous consequence of unrestricted competition is that it yields intuitive, but not obvious, results. When buyers have plenty of choices, your potential for profit depends on the number of buyers who believe that your product or service is "better" than your competitors' products or services. As we saw, "better" doesn't necessarily mean that you have either the better product or the lowest costs. Rather, it is your ability to create more value with the buyer than any other company could—a measure succinctly described by your company's value-gap advantage.

Furthermore, an understanding of value-gap advantages explains how competing firms can coexist profitably. Competition may be brutal, but as long as the firms' products are not a pure commodity, there can be many ways for different companies to make money. The key lies first in understanding how buyer preferences differ, and then in tailoring your company's value-gap advantages to specific buyer segments.

Having covered the basic theory in parts I through III of this book, we were then able to discuss the art of identifying relevant players—step 1 above—in part IV. We were also able to discuss the art of assessing the sustainability of profits—step 4—in part V. The good news is that understanding sustainability does not require any new theory. But it does require additional judgments—judgments about whether new players will enter, about whether existing players will improve, and about whether buyer preferences and suppliers' costs will change. As always, the theory points you to the judgments that you need to make, but of course, it can't make the judgments for you. You must make them.

Step 3 is self-explanatory. Ideally, you want to be able to be profitable under unrestricted competition. But in some cases competition may be restricted, thus opening up additional possibilities for profit. There is no general theory for profitability under *restricted* competition, but we considered examples from three important forms of restricted competition: firms choosing not to compete unrestrictedly, firms prevented from competing unrestrictedly, and firms not knowing enough to compete unrestrictedly.

Finally, there is the question of whether you should try to change the game—step 5. Instead of changing the game, you might only want to play it differently. For instance, if competition is only partially determining the division of value, it may be that your firm could bargain more effectively for the remaining value. However, you might actually want to change the game—that is, make strategic moves that change the structure of the environment in which you compete. This topic is broad enough for another entire book, so, in part V, I only presented some examples, including making decisions on entry and positioning and creating competition. Additionally, I show how integrating strategic moves into a value-based analysis provides an important insight for business: the inevitable possibility of coordination failure and management's role in preventing it.

Here is the main point that I want you to take from this book: business has been successfully transacted for millennia, and while modern business transactions can seem hopelessly complex, you needn't throw your hands up in despair. You know a great deal about business—especially your own business. Use your knowledge. Use it in tandem with a theory that respects that knowledge—the theory of a value-based analysis—because no one is in a better position than you are to develop a successful strategy for your business.

Notes

Part I

The theory in this book applies cooperative game theory to business strategy. Early versions of this work are in sections 1–5 of Brandenburger and Stuart (1996) and in Stuart (2001).

Treating price as a consequence of competition has a long history. My decision to start with this perspective was influenced by the work of Louis Makowski and Joe Ostroy (e.g., see Makowski and Ostroy 2001), an observation by Elon Kohlberg, and Edgeworth (1881).

In chapter 2, the term "value gap" is due to David Collis. In the appendix to chapter 2, the term "unrestricted competition" describes the core of a cooperative game. The core is due to Gillies (1959), and the reasoning behind the core appears in Edgeworth (1881). The choice of the phrase "unrestricted competition" is due, in part, to the phrase "unbridled competition" in Aumann (1985: 53).

In chapter 3, the need to define willingness to pay and economic cost based on options "outside" of the game is from section 4 of Brandenburger and Stuart (1996).

Part II

Chapters 4 and 5 are based on lemma 3 in Stuart (2004) and proposition 1 in Stuart (2016).

Part III

Chapters 6 to 11 are based on sections 2, 3.2, and 3.3 in Stuart (2016).

The monopoly and supply–demand results in the appendix to chapter 6 are standard results from cooperative game theory. In particular, see Kaneko (1976). For papers that embed these results in a context with explicit capacity choices, see Stuart (2007) and Stuart (2005).

Part IV

In chapter 13, the right-hand side of figure 13.1 is from Brandenburger and Stuart (1996). The left-hand side is from teaching materials developed by Scott Borg and Adam Brandenburger. For a formal result using buyers, firms, and suppliers, see Stuart (1997).

In chapter 14, the special category of firm complements corresponds to the complements category in Brandenburger and Nalebuff's (1996) value net.

In chapter 15, the example regarding the willingness to pay for TV is based on "Would you take $1,000,000 to give up TV forever?" (*TV Guide*, October 10–16, 1992: 11–12.) Using physical location to illustrate that relative value creation does not imply arbitrary value creation is due to Scott Borg. Fact 1 is a standard result for the core of a cooperative game; see, for example, remark 2.3 in Moulin (1995). Fact 2 follows from fact 1 and theorem 5 in Aumann and Dreze (1974).

Part V

The specific barriers to entry listed in chapter 16 are drawn from the standard strategy literature. The decision about which examples to include was greatly influenced by discussions with Bruce Greenwald and by his book, Greenwald and Kahn (2005).

The examples at the end of chapter 16 are due to Cory Williamson. The oil rig example was inspired by a ball-bearing example from Scott Borg.

Chapter 17 relies on the biform game formalism from Brandenburger and Stuart (2007). The game in figure 17.7 is motivated by Adam Brandenburger's example regarding Jaguar automobiles. The game in figure 17.12 is based on example 2.2 in Brandenburger and Stuart (2007).

The result at the end of chapter 17 is based on proposition D1 in Brandenburger and Stuart (2006).

The game of figure 18.4 is adapted from a "Judo" strategy example from Adam Brandenburger. The example is motivated by Gelman and Salop (1983).

References

Aumann, R. 1985. What is game theory trying to accomplish? In *Frontiers of Economics*, ed. K. J. Arrow and S. Honkapohja, 28–76. Oxford: Basil Blackwell.

Aumann, R., and J. Dreze. 1974. Cooperative games with coalition structures. *International Journal of Game Theory* 3: 217–37.

Brandenburger, Adam, and Barry Nalebuff. 1996. *Co-opetition*. New York: Doubleday.

Brandenburger, Adam, and H. W. Stuart Jr. 1996. Value-based business strategy. *Journal of Economics and Management Strategy* 5 (1): 5–24.

Brandenburger, Adam, and H. W. Stuart, Jr. 2006. Biform Games: Additional Online Material. Unpublished manuscript.

Brandenburger, Adam, and H. W. Stuart, Jr. 2007. Biform games. *Management Science* 53: 537–49.

Edgeworth, F. Y. 1881. *Mathematical Psychics: An Essay on the Mathematics to the Moral Sciences.* London: Kegan Paul.

Gelman, J., and S. Salop. 1983. Judo economics: Capacity limitation and coupon competition. *Bell Journal of Economics* 14: 315–25.

Gillies, D. B. 1959. Solutions to general non–zero-sum games. In *Contributions to the Theory of Games IV (Annals of Mathematics Studies 40)*, ed. A. W. Tucker and R. D. Luce, 47–85. Princeton: Princeton University Press.

Greenwald, Bruce C., and Judd Kahn. 2005. *Competition Demystified: A Radically Simplified Approach to Business Strategy.* New York: Penguin Group.

Kaneko, M. 1976. On the core and competitive equilibria of a market with indivisible goods. *Naval Research Logistics Quarterly* 23: 321–37.

Makowski, L. and J. Ostroy. 2001. Perfect competition and the creativity of the market. *Journal of Economic Literature* 39: 479–535.

Moulin, H. 1995. *Cooperative Microeconomics: A Game-Theoretic Introduction.* Princeton: Princeton University Press.

Stuart, H. W., Jr. 1997. The Supplier–Firm–Buyer game and its M-sided generalization. *Mathematical Social Sciences* 34: 21–27.

Stuart, H. W., Jr. 2001. Cooperative games and business strategy. In *Game Theory and Business Applications*, ed. K. Chatterjee and W. F. Samuelson, 189–211. Boston: Kluwer.

Stuart, H. W., Jr. 2004. Efficient spatial competition. *Games and Economic Behavior* 49: 345–62.

Stuart, H. W., Jr. 2005. Biform analysis of inventory competition. *Manufacturing and Service Operations Management* 7 (4): 347–59.

Stuart, H. W., Jr. 2007. Creating monopoly power. *International Journal of Industrial Organization* 25: 1011–25.

Stuart, H. W., Jr. 2016. Value gaps and profitability. *Strategy Science* 1 (1): 56–70.

Index

Bargaining, 6
  competition and, 13–14, 17–19
  monopoly power and, 72
Barriers to entry
  buyer-side, 162–63
  competitors and, 172–73
  cost or supplier-side, 163–65
Boundaries, game, 152–53
Bounds
  economic cost, 37–38
  salary premiums and discounts, 38–39
  willingness to pay, 29–30
Branding, 162, 163
Buyers
  envious, 81–84, 98–101
  firm complements and, 141–45
  identifying, 120–23
  impact of excluded buyers on contributed
    values of included, 66–67
  inclusion in the game, 120–23
  introductory prices and new, 172
  market size and, 125
  profitability and excluded, 63–66
  relevance of, 118–19
  search costs, 162
  segments, 53–56, 126
  segments with excess demand, 113–14
  simplified game, 124–25
  switching costs, 162
  value created with, 45–48

  willingness to pay (*see* Willingness to pay
    (WTP))

Capacity
  constraint, marginal cost as, 89–90
  market-price effects and available, 107
Causal ambiguity, 163, 164–65
Change, strategic, 173–76
Compensated willingness to pay, 82–84, 97
Competency, 163, 164–65
Competition
  bargaining and, 13–14, 17–19
  economies of scale and, 90–93
  exclusion benefits for, 68–69
  implying efficiency, 22–23
  interdependency of, 56–57
  mathematics of unrestricted, 20–21
  monopoly as one-sided, 70–74
  for new buyer segments, 169–72
  price-setting power and, 67–68
  restricted, 19
  restricted due to firm choices, 191–93
  restricted due to lack of information,
    194
  restricted due to law or social convention,
    193–94
  strategic decisions creating, 176–79
  supply and demand as two-sided, 74–78
  unrestricted, 10–13, 20–24
Competitive condition, 21–22

Competitors
  barriers to entry, 172–73
  defined, 119–20
  firm complements and, 141–45
  identifying, 120–23
  inclusion in the game, 120–23, 136–37
  suppliers and, 135–37
Complementarity, 145–46
Complements, firm, 141–45
Constant marginal costs, 50, 104
Consumers. *See* Buyers
Contributed value, 8–9
  boundaries of game and, 153
  impact of excluded buyer on, 66–67
  perspective, 23–24
  value-gap advantages and, 58–60
Coordination failures, 183–86
  with incentive alignment and no
      externalities, 186–88
Cost(s), 4. *See also* Economic cost
  barriers to entry, 163–65
  constant marginal, 50
  economic, 4, 33–38, 39–41
  economies of scale and, 90–93
  guaranteed profitability and increased
      marginal, 85–87
  marginal, 50, 85–93
  nonconstant marginal, 103–104
  opportunity, 4
  production, 34–35
  search, 162
  seller's, 5–6, 33–34
  supplier, 127–29, 141–45
  switching, 162

Demand
  being in, 106, 109
  buyer segment with excess, 113–14
  curve, 69–70
  market-price effects and, 109–11
  market-price intuition and, 95–96
  and supply as two-sided competition, 74–78
  sustainability and excess, 165

Differentiation, 48–52
Discounts, price, 31, 32
  inferring bounds on, 31

Economic cost, 4, 33–34
  not necessarily production cost, 34–35
  revealed preference and, 37–38
  as subjective, 35–37
  using decision trees in calculating, 39–41
Economies of scale, 90–93
  as barrier to entry, 163–64
Efficiency, competition and, 22–23
Enter *vs.* don't enter decision, 173–74
Envious buyers, 81–82
  compensated willingness to pay and, 82–84
  market-price effects creating, 98–101
Excess demand, 165
Exclusion, 63–66
  benefiting all competitors, 68–69
  impact on contributed values of included
      buyers, 66–67
  marginal cost as capacity constraint and,
      89–90
  monopoly power and, 69–74
  potential profits and, 104–106
  supply and demand as two-sided
      competition and, 75–76
  supply exceeding demand and, 79–80
  willingness to pay demand curve and, 69–70
Externalities and incentives with strategic
      decisions, 186–88

Feasibility condition, 21–22
Firms. *See* Competitors
Fixed outside option, 27–28

Game matrix, 182–83, 188–90
Games, business, 7–14
  boundaries of, 149–53
  broader perspective on players in, 123–24
  buyers in, 118–19
  competition and bargaining, 13–14
  competitors in, 119–20, 136–37

contributed value and, 8–9
introducing competition to, 9–10
market size and, 125
multiple stages in, 139–41
simplification, 124–25
strategic moves for changing, 169–90
suppliers in, 134–35, 136–37
unrestricted competition, 10–13
Guaranteed price, 68, 82, 88, 97, 101, 109–10
Guaranteed profitability, 63–78, 83–84, 103, 114

Habits, buyer, 162, 163

Incentives and externalities with strategic decisions, 186–88
Interaction of strategic moves, 179–83
Interdependency of competition, 56–57
Introductory prices, 172
Intuition, market-price, 95–96

Lack of information, competition restricted due to, 194
Law or social convention, competition restricted due to, 193–94

Marginal costs
  as capacity constraint, 89–90
  constant, 50, 104
  economies of scale and, 90–93
  guaranteed profitability and, 85–87
  nonconstant, 103–104
  prices set equal to, 87–88
  value creation and, 88–89
Market-price effects, 95
  compensated willingness to pay and, 97
  creating envious buyers, 98–101
  market-price intuition and, 95–96
  potential profitability and, 106–108
  willingness to pay and, 96
Market size, 125
Monopoly power, 69–74
Multiple stages in the game, 139–41

One-sided competition, monopoly as, 70–74
Opportunity cost, 4
Outcome matrix, 179–81

Patents, 163, 164
Payoff analysis, 169–72
Potential price, 110–11
Potential profits, 57–58, 114
  exclusion and, 104–106
  market-price effects and, 106–108
  minimum and maximum estimates of, 108–109
Preference, revealed, 29–30, 37–38
Premium, price, 30
  inferring bounds on, 31
  not larger than a WTP advantage, 31–32
Prices
  as a consequence, 17
  discounts, 31, 32
  guaranteed, 68, 82, 88, 97, 101, 109–10
  introductory, 172
  potential, 110–11
  premium and willingness to pay, 30, 31–32
  price-setting as strategic move, 172
  price-setting power, 67–68
  set equal to marginal cost, 87–88
  translating between value capture and, 16–17
  value capture and, 16–17, 131
  walkaway, 3
  willingness to pay and, 26–27, 31–32
Production cost, 34–35
Products
  branding, 162, 163
  consumer willingness to pay for, 29
  differentiation, cost, and profitability, 48–52
  disappearing demand for, 165–67
  modifications as strategic change, 174–76
  switching costs, 162
Profitability
  assessing sustainability of, 160–65
  enter vs. don't enter decision and, 173–74
  envious buyers and, 81–84

Profitability (cont.)
  excluded buyer and, 63–66, 68–69
  flows, 132–34
  guaranteed, 63–78, 83–84, 103, 114
  increasing marginal costs and guaranteed,
    85–87
  low cost, differentiation, and, 48–52
  market-price effects and, 106–108
  path to understanding, 196
  potential, 57–58, 104–109, 114
  price-setting power and, 67–68
  sustainable, 157–67
  value creation and, 3–6
  willingness to pay and, 3–5, 25

Restricted competition, 19
  due to firm choices, 191–93
  due to lack of information, 194
  due to law or social convention, 193–94
Revealed preference, 29–30, 37–38

Salary premiums
  bounds on, 38–39
  revealed preference and, 37–38
Search costs, 162
Segments, buyer, 53–56, 126
  competing for new, 169–71, *172*
  with excess demand, 113–14
  suppliers and, 127–31
  sustainability of profits and, 160–62
Smith, Adam, 187
Strategic decisions
  barriers to entry and, 172–73
  competition restricted due to firm choices
    and, 191–93
  competition restricted due to lack of
    information, 194
  competition restricted due to law or social
    convention and, 193–94
  coordination failure and, 183–86
  creating competition, 176–79
  enter *vs.* don't enter, 173–74
  game matrix and, 182–83, 188–90

incentives and externalities, 186–88
  interaction of, 179–83
  price-setting, 172
  uncertainty and strategic change, 174–76
Subjectivity
  in value creation, 150–52
  in willingness to pay, 28
Suppliers, 127–31
  accounted for in and out of the game,
    135
  competitors and, 135–37
  firm complements and, 141–45
  inclusion in the game, 134–35
  profit flow and, 132–34
  and supply-side barriers to entry, 163–65
  value creation and, 129–31
  value gaps with, 131–32
Supply
  and demand as two sided competition,
    74–78
  marginal cost as capacity constraint and,
    89–90
  market-price effects and, 109–11
Sustainability, 157–58
  barriers to entry and, 162–65
  excess demand and, 165
  of the pie, 158–60
  of profits, 160–65
  when the pie is disappearing, 165–67
Switching costs, 162

Total value creation (TVC), 6. *See also* Value
    creation
  and players' choices maximizing, 187
Two-sided competition, supply and demand
    as, 74–78

Uncertainty and strategic change, 174–76
Unrestricted competition, 10–13
  competitive condition and feasibility
    condition, 21–22
  contributed value perspective, 23–24
  mathematics of, 20–24

Value
  capture and prices, 16–17, 131
  complementarity, 141–46
  contributed, 8–9, 23–24, 58–60, 66–67, 153
Value creation, 3–6
  with the customer, 45–48
  firm complements and, 141–46
  marginal, 88–89
  as relative, 147–50
  shrinking, 165–67
  subjectivity of, 150–52
  suppliers and, 129–31
Value gap, 13–18
Value-gap advantage (VGA), 45–52, 196–97
  by buyer segment, 54–56
  buyer segments with excess demand and,
    113–14
  constant marginal costs and, 88–89, 104
  contributed value and, 58–60
  envious buyers and, 81–84
  excluded buyers and, 80–81
  finding buyer segments with, 113
  nonconstant marginal costs and, 103–104
  potential profits and, 57–58
  with suppliers, 131–132
  value creation with customer and, 45–48

Walkaway price, 3
Willingness to pay (WTP), 3–5
  based on best outside alternative, 33
  as benchmark for buyer profit, 25
  calculating, 26–27
  compensated, 82–84, 97
  for consumer product, 29
  contributed value and, 8–9
  demand curve, 69–70
  envy and compensated, 82–84
  excluded buyers and, 63–66
  firm complements and, 141–45
  fixed outside option, 27–28
  inferring bounds on, 29–30
  market-price effect and, 96
  multiple stages and, 139–41

  potential net benefit and, 7
  price discounts and, 31, 32
  price premiums and, 30, 31–32
  subjectivity in, 28
  subjectivity of value creation and, 150–52
  sustainability of profits and, 160–65
  sustainability of the pie and, 158–60
  unrestricted competition and, 10–13
  using decision trees in calculating, 39–41
WTP. See Willingness to pay (WTP)